THE GOLDEN CALF   21

Story: Exodus 32   Memory: Exodus 20:3

Moses had climbed to the top of Mount Sinai to receive the Ten Commandments. While he was away, Moses left his brother, Aaron, in charge of the Israelites. Moses had been on the mountain for a very long time. Some of the Israelites were tired of waiting and became very impatient. They wanted to worship a god they could see. To make the Israelites happy, Aaron told the people to give him all of their gold jewelry. Aaron melted the gold and made an idol that looked like a calf. The Israelites started praying to the golden calf. They thanked the idol, instead of God, for leading them out of Egypt. When Moses came back down the mountain, he saw the people praying to this golden calf. Moses was so angry with the Israelites for disobeying that he threw the tablets onto the ground, and they shattered into many pieces.

1. Who did Moses put in charge of the Israelites?
2. Why did the Israelites want a golden idol?
3. What did the people thank the golden calf for?
4. How did the Israelites disobey God?
5. How did Moses react to the golden calf?
6. Why should we worship only God?

BibleStoryCards™   © 1995 WPH   1-800-493-7539

OLD TESTAMENT

Storytelling & Review Guide

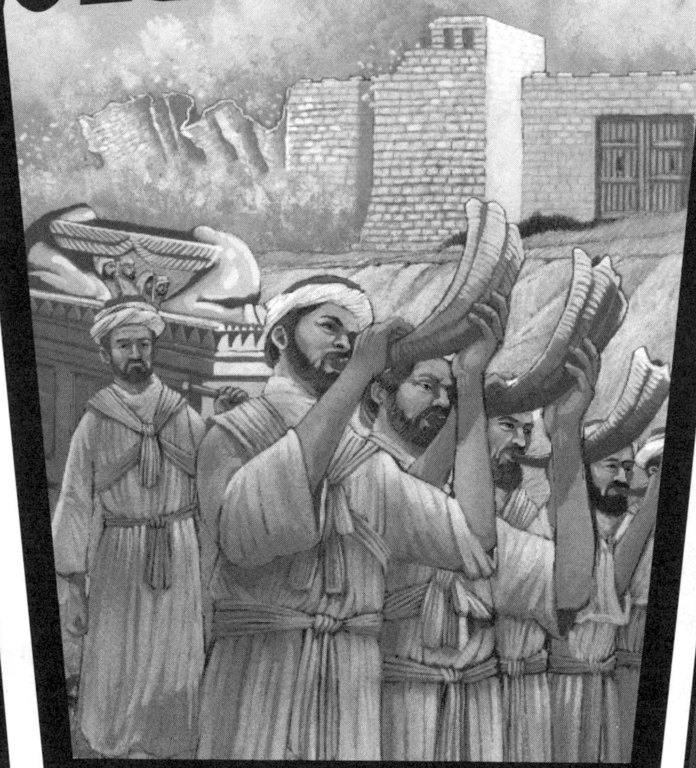

WENDY WAGONER AND GARY SWYERS

Editorial Staff
Wendy Wagoner, Editor
Gary Swyers, Managing Editor
Kelly Trennepohl, General Editor
David Higle, Senior Editor
Special thanks to those who served on various committees providing encouragement, ideas, and direction. Also, thanks to those who gave input to the review and memory games.

Copyright © 2006 by Wesleyan Publishing House
All Rights Reserved
Published by Wesleyan Publishing House
Indianapolis, Indiana 46250
Printed in the United States of America
ISBN 0-89827-150-9

Scripture taken from the HOLY BIBLE, NEW INTERNATIONAL VERSION®. NIV. Copyright 1973, 1978, 1984 by International Bible Society. Used by permission of Zondervan Publishing House. All rights reserved.

All rights reserved. No part of this publication may be reproduced, stored in a retrieval system, or transmitted in any form or by any means — electronic, mechanical, photocopy, recording or any other — except for brief quotations in printed reviews, without the prior written permission of the publisher.

CONTENTS

BEFORE YOU BEGIN

How to Use the STORYTELLING & REVIEW GUIDE™ 5

How to Use Bible Story Cards. 7

Before You Tell a Story 9

Storytelling Tips 11

Telling a Story in Morning Worship Service 13

STORIES

1 Creation. 15	26 Crossing the Jordan. 40
2 The First Sin 16	27 Fall of Jericho 41
3 Cain & Abel 17	28 Achan 42
4 Noah's Ark 18	29 Gideon. 43
5 Tower of Babel 19	30 Samson 44
6 Sodom & Gomorrah 20	31 Ruth & Naomi. 45
7 Abraham Offers Isaac 21	32 Samuel's Call 46
8 Jacob & Esau 22	33 Samuel Anoints Saul. 47
9 Jacob Wrestles With God 23	34 Samuel Anoints David 48
10 Joseph's Coat 24	35 David & Goliath 49
11 Joseph in Prison 25	36 David Spares Saul. 50
12 Joseph Rules in Egypt. 26	37 Return of the Ark 51
13 Baby Moses. 27	38 Building the Temple 52
14 The Burning Bush. 28	39 Ravens Feed Elijah 53
15 The Plagues. 29	40 Fire From Heaven. 54
16 The First Passover. 30	41 Naaman 55
17 Crossing the Red Sea 31	42 Joash 56
18 Eating Manna 32	43 Job. 57
19 Moses Strikes the Rock 33	44 Jonah 58
20 The Ten Commandments 34	45 Isaiah's Vision. 59
21 The Golden Calf 35	46 Jeremiah 60
22 The Tabernacle 36	47 The Fiery Furnace. 61
23 Twelve Spies. 37	48 Daniel 62
24 The Bronze Snake. 38	49 Esther 63
25 Balaam's Donkey 39	50 Rebuilding the Wall 64

CONTENTS continued

STORYTELLING AND REVIEW RESOURCES

Storytelling Methods 67
Review Questions and Answers 71
Additional Review Questions 81
Memory Verse List 91
Memory Verse Cards 93
Storyteller Memory Object List 99
Character Descriptions 101
Review Games and Activities 107
Memory Verse Games and Activities 113
Memory Object Games and Activities 119
Charts and Maps
    The Old Testament Bookshelf 121
    When Old Testament Events Happened 122
    Rulers of Israel & Judah 123
    Times of the Prophets 124
    Land of Abraham 125
    The Exodus 126
    Bible Lands 127
    Where It All Happened 128
    Moses & the Exodus 129
    The Tabernacle 130
    The Ten Commandments 131
    Conquest of Canaan 132
    Joshua Entering the Land of Canaan 133
    David's Conquests 134
    Jerusalem 135
    Temple 136
    Solomon's Temple 137

HOW TO USE THE Storytelling & Review Guide™

This guide is designed to provide a variety of storytelling methods with maximum flexiblity. You will enjoy the easy-to-use sections. The first section consists of 50 Storytelling lessons, one page per story. The second section, Storytelling & Review Resources is packed with ideas, tips, questions, memory verse cards, games, maps, and charts to enhance your storytelling skills. This last section has plenty of reproducible pages for use in storytelling, review, or to give to parents for reinforcing the stories at home.

The Storytelling and Review Guide™ lessons are divided into two different sections: Storytelling Time, and Review & Memory Time. The individual parts of each section are described below:

STORYTELLING TIME

1. TO THE STORYTELLER — This part is specifically for the storyteller. It helps the storyteller to get a feel for the main focus or principle of the story.

2. STORYTELLING METHODS — This part gives three different ways or methods for telling the story. A detailed description of a particular method can be found on the page number listed by the method. The methods listed are options, of course; each individual storyteller may have a particular method of storytelling.

3. MEMORY OBJECT — Each story will suggest a memory object that the storyteller can show at some point in the story. These objects are mental hooks that will help the children to remember the story.

4. REVIEW QUESTIONS — The questions from the back of the Bible story card (with their answers) are listed in this section for easy reference.

5. PRAYER FOCUS — This section will have a suggested prayer emphasis to end your storytelling time.

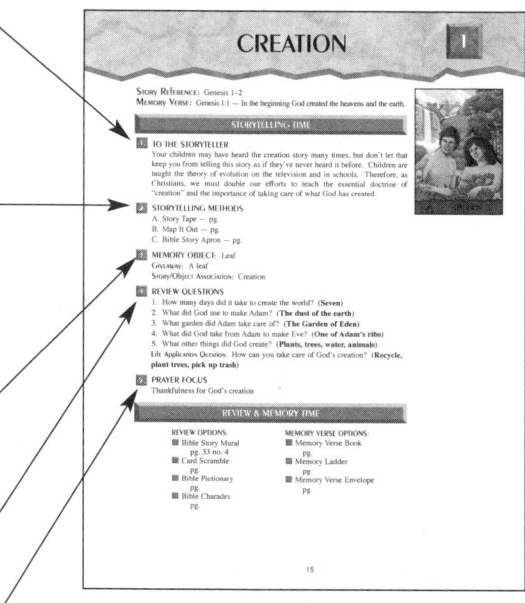

REVIEW & MEMORY TIME

REVIEW OPTIONS — This section lists suggested game ideas for review. The page number listed beside each game refers you to a detailed description of how the game is to be played. You are encouraged to use games that you know will work for your children.

5

MEMORY TIME OPTIONS — This section lists Memory Verse and Memory Object game ideas. Memory time is used specifically for reviewing stories, and to see how much the children remember. The page number listed beside each memory time idea refers you to a description of how to review using this method.

In the Storytelling & Review resource section you will notice the following icons:

These icons help to quickly indentify each storytelling resource. Just look for the icon which corresponds with the desired resource.

HOW TO USE BibleStoryCards™

Most curriculum efforts today are spent in application and activities, and not on Bible stories. BibleStoryCards™ give teachers sequential Bible stories and are based on stories children ought to know. They are perfect for adding to the following programs:

Sunday school	**home schooling**
Vacation Bible School	**Christian day school**
midweek programs	**children's sermon**
children's church	**family devotions**

By adding BibleStoryCards™ to your existing program, Bible learning is enhanced. And since this curriculum is built on a "back to basics" approach, there is plenty of fun memorization, as well as exciting review ideas.

Each story has a full page of helpful information to guide you through a successful story time. Plus, the Resource Pages provide a wealth of additional helps for each session, including memory and review games, activities, charts, maps, and parents pages. Many of the Resource Pages can be photocopied.

BibleStoryCards™ will intiate or renew your children's interest in Bible stories, and will guide you in the age-old learning method of storytelling.

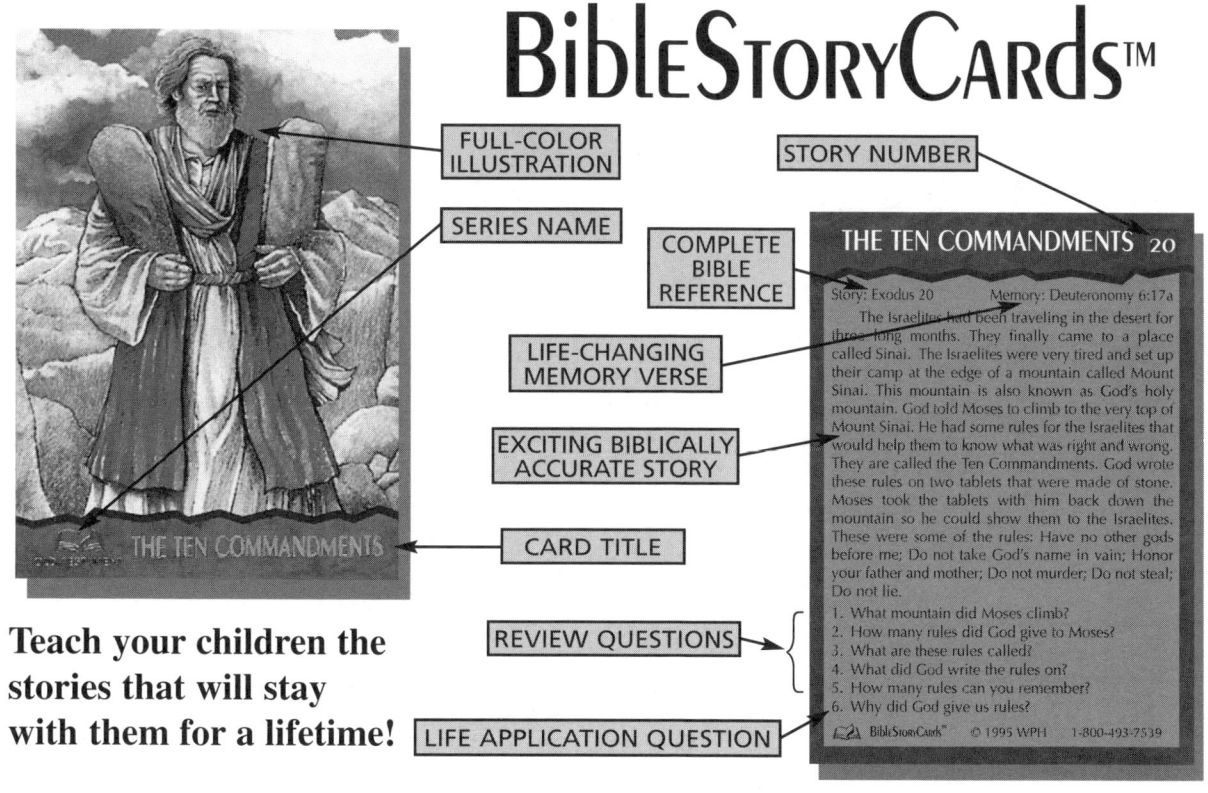

Teach your children the stories that will stay with them for a lifetime!

BEFORE YOU TELL A STORY

1. **ALWAYS** prepare for your stories. In order for your storytelling to be as effective as it can be, you must take some time to prepare.

   a. Each day, read through your story two or three different times. If you do this, you should be very familiar with the story before you have to tell it.

   b. Practice different intonations of your voice. Don't strain your voice, but fluctuate it when you tell the story, especially when you are speaking in an older person's or a child's voice.

   c. Practice your facial expressions. If there is a scary part in the story, have a scared look on your face. If one of the characters in the story is angry, have an angry expression on your face. Also, make sure your voice indicates anger.

   d. Stand in front of a mirror and practice telling your story. Use this practice time to work on your facial expressions and voice intonations.

2. **NEVER** read a story word for word, unless you are narrating (see page 70, #14). If it isn't easy for you to tell a story from memory, jot down some notes on a small index card. You can write down some key points that will help you remember the progression of the story.

3. Make sure that you can be **seen easily** by all of the children. If you don't have a platform to stand on, make sure that you move around a lot so all of the children can see you. Another possibility may be to have the children sit on the floor while you stand and tell the story.

4. Make sure that you can be **heard easily** by all of the children. You may need to hold a microphone while you tell the story. It would be beneficial to have a clip-on microphone so that your hands would be free to hold the object that goes along with the story.

5. As you tell the story, make eye contact with the children and show a lot of enthusiasm. This brings the children into the story with you. When they know that you enjoy telling the story, it is more interesting and enjoyable for them. It also helps to eliminate some discipline problems.

6. It is all right to stop in the middle of your story and ask the children questions. This keeps them on their toes. If you are telling the story about Abraham offering Isaac, ask them how they think Abraham felt when God asked him to sacrifice his son. You could even ask them how they would have felt if they had been in Isaac's shoes. Would they have been as brave as he was?

7. When you are telling a very familiar story, one that most of your children have heard several times, like David and Goliath, try doing some research and dig up specific details that would make the story more interesting and seem new again. For instance, research the Philistines. Find out what type of armor the men in the Philistine army wore, and maybe bring in a picture to show the children. Older children would be very interested in these details.

STORYTELLING TIPS

Principles for Effective Storytelling

Storytelling scares more new teachers than perhaps any other facet of teaching. The prospect of having to capture the interest of squirming children and then sustain that interest for the duration of a story seems like a greater challenge than many people are ready to face.

Fortunately, effective storytelling is a skill that anyone can develop by practicing a few simple principles:

Have Confidence in Your Story

Why is this story worth hearing? Ask yourself this question to be sure you are clear on the value of the story to your class. People will listen to a story that offers them a benefit.

Ask yourself: What is the most interesting thing about this story? What are the features of this story that compel attention? What will my class be drawn to as they listen?

A few moments spent answering these questions can help you build confidence in the value and appeal of your story. When you are confident that the story has value and appeal, then you will be less concerned about your storytelling ability.

Prepare and Practice Your Story

Four essential steps should be taken in getting ready to tell any story:

Identify where the story is going. If you are clear about the purpose of the story, you will be less likely to wander off the track. Your curriculum provides a lesson focus to help you identify the story's main point.

Outline the story or read the outline provided in your curriculum, identifying the major events that occur.

Review the story facts enough so that each point in the outline will remind you of the details involved in that event.

Practice telling the story aloud using your outline to prompt you from one main point to the next. Tell your story to someone in your family, to a tape recorder or to yourself in the mirror.

Capture Interest at the Start

A good beginning is essential, because it is much easier to capture an audience than it is to recapture them after their attention has wandered. The surest way to kill interest is to ask, "Does anybody remember last week's story?" If this week's story connects in any way to last week's story, you can jog your children's memories as you proceed.

The best way to begin most stories with children is through some type of experience interesting to everyone in the group. This experience needs to connect to some aspect of the story. The younger your children, the more crucial it is to start a story with a reference to something in their own experience:

Ask a question about something you know your children have seen or done. For example, to introduce the story of the wise men who followed the star, ask children to briefly tell of a time they looked up into a nighttime sky. Share your own experience to give children some insights into your life.

11

Share a *brief* illustration to introduce your story. This could be an incident from your own experience, something recently reported in the news, or something you have read. Bible story time is the focal point of every session. Unfortunately, too many teachers wind up boring young children during the Bible story time because they do not work on simple basic guidelines to good storytelling.

Guideline #1 — Teach from the Bible, not your curriculum.

Children need to see you as a teacher of God's Word—not merely a reader of a curriculum product. Have your open Bible in front of you throughout the story, and clearly state that the story is true: "It really happened to real people."

Guideline #2 — Know your story

well enough to talk *with* your students rather than read *to* them. Make simple notes to help you remember and properly sequence the three or four most important events. When your eyes are not tied to the words of the story, you are free to focus on the faces of the children in your class. By *telling* rather than *reading* the story, you will be better able to express enthusiasm through your face and voice. Knowing the story well also enables you to freely use your hands to move any Bible story figures on the flannel board.

Guideline #3 — Ask good questions

at the beginning and end of a story. Young children need to hear a logical flow in the story line. Since their attention is easily diverted, they need to hear a story from beginning to end without interruptions in order to understand it. Decide what you want children to focus on in the story. Ask them to listen for that before you begin telling the story (e.g., "In our story today, listen to find out what God wanted David to do.") Then at the end of the story, ask them to give you the information from the story they just heard (e.g., "What did God want David to do in our story?") Asking questions in this way helps children discover information on their own. And children will remember what they discover for themselves longer than the things they merely hear us tell them.

Guideline #4 — Emphasize the main goal of the Bible story character.

This element is the key to being able to recall information in the story. Clearly define the main goal of the principal character in your story. Emphasize this goal when you tell the story. By your emphasis, children's ability to recall the main goal will increase dramatically.

Guideline #5 — Practice.

Take time to practice telling your Bible stories out loud! Use a cassette tape recorder, practice occasionally with another teacher from your department, tell the story to a family member, or even practice storytelling in front of a mirror. Be sure that you are giving your best to God and to the children He has entrusted to you.

Sunday School Smart Pages by Wes & Sheryl Haystead
© Copyright 1992 by Gospel Light
Regal Books, Ventura, CA 93003
Used by Permission

TELLING A STORY IN MORNING WORSHIP SERVICE

1. Stick to the time slot.

The single most important factor in telling the story during morning worship service is to stick to the four- or five-minute time slot — never, ever going over six minutes. The four- or five-minute time slot is about the same length as a special song and can serve as a component of a morning worship service. A time slot over six minutes will not survive permanently as a part of the worship service, so make sure you can tell the story simply and to the point. Don't embellish it to the extent that you have to "tell it all"; simply give the sketch for the story and follow up on it later in children's church or somewhere else.

2. Talk to the kids, not the adults.

Your back to the audience. The congregation wants to see the kids, not you. Make sure you tell the story to the children, and not the adults. Use a microphone so the adults can hear, but let the children's faces — not yours — be the focus. Don't worry. The adults will get plenty out of it, too.

3. Give a memory object.

If you are doing a follow-up in children's church, still give out a memory object during the storytelling time in worship service. It isn't necessary to have a "Giveaway" object each week, but it is nice to do this from time to time. If you don't have an object to hand out to each child, at least have one for the children to look at.

4. Hand out the cards.

To move the story along speedily, consider handing out the cards at the beginning of the story, rather than at the end. Sure, the children will glance down and study the card while you are telling the story — go ahead and let them. They'll learn that much more from the picture.

5. Ask a few questions.

You will seldom be able to ask more than three or four questions, but occasionally as many as six. Be careful about asking too many review questions about "last week's story," for a minute can disappear quickly when you are up front. At least try to ask a final tie-down review question on the story you just told.

6. Take turns.

Though there may be only one or two storytellers in the congregation, try to recruit other storytellers to help you. Some pastors guard this time jealously for its effect on both children and parents and the overall communication that "this pastor cares for children." But even in this case, at least one other person should be brought in from time to time as a "relief pitcher."

7. Don't tell everything.

There simply is not enough time to tell an elaborate story. In using the Bible Story Cards curriculum during a morning worship, all you are doing is giving a "thumbnail summary" of a Bible story. Your real job is to create hunger and interest in the entire story. That's where the card comes in — to ignite parents to tell the story in greater detail. And then, of course, there is always children's church and other programs of the church where the story can be expanded and the details can be filled in. Don't get frustrated that you are leaving a lot unsaid. This is how pastors feel at the end of every message — but you just can't "say it all," or the service would go on forever!

CREATION

STORY REFERENCE: Genesis 1 – 2
MEMORY VERSE: Genesis 1:1 — In the beginning God created the heavens and the earth.

STORYTELLING TIME

1. TO THE STORYTELLER
Your children may have heard the creation story many times, but don't let that keep you from telling this story as if they've never heard it before. Children are taught the theory of evolution on the television and in schools. Therefore, as Christians, we must double our efforts to teach the essential doctrine of "creation" and the importance of taking care of what God has created.

2. STORYTELLING METHODS
A. Story Tape — pg. 67, #1
B. Map It Out — pg. 67, #4
C. Bible Story Apron — pg. 69, #10

3. MEMORY OBJECT: Leaf
GIVEAWAY: A leaf
STORY/OBJECT ASSOCIATION: Creation

4. REVIEW QUESTIONS
1. How many days did it take to create the world? (**Seven**)
2. What did God use to make Adam? (**The dust of the earth**)
3. What garden did Adam take care of? (**The Garden of Eden**)
4. What did God take from Adam to make Eve? (**One of Adam's ribs**)
5. What other things did God create? (**Plants, trees, water, animals**)

LIFE APPLICATION QUESTION: How can you take care of God's creation? (**Recycle, plant trees, pick up trash**)

5. PRAYER FOCUS
Thankfulness for God's creation

REVIEW & MEMORY TIME

REVIEW OPTIONS:
- Card Scramble
  pg. 107, #1
- Bible Pictionary
  pg. 108, #9
- Bible Charades
  pg. 109, #14
- Bible Story Mural
  pg. 111, #26

MEMORY VERSE OPTIONS:
- Memory Verse Book
  pg. 113, #1
- Memory Verse Envelope
  pg. 113, #3
- Memory Ladder
  pg. 116, #16

2 THE FIRST SIN

THE FIRST SIN

Story Reference: Genesis 3
Memory Verse: 1 John 1:9 — If we confess our sins, he is faithful and just and will forgive us our sins and purify us from all unrighteousness.

STORYTELLING TIME

1. TO THE STORYTELLER
BEFORE YOU BEGIN: Ask review questions from the previous story.
When teaching children, many people try to "soften" the word *sin* because to them it sounds harsh. Don't hesitate to call it what it is; sin is sin and it is something of which we have all been guilty. The modern world often teaches that each person has his own definition of right and wrong. Whatever feels right for him is right, no matter what it may be. What will happen to our world if there are no absolutes? Through this story, children should learn that anytime we consciously decide to disregard or disobey what God has commanded, we have sinned and need to ask for His forgiveness.

2. STORYTELLING METHODS
A. Draw a Picture — pg. 68, #7
B. Bible Story Cards — pg. 69, #11
C. Narration — pg. 70, #14

3. MEMORY OBJECT: A piece of fruit
Giveaway: A small apple
Story/Object Association: The forbidden fruit that Adam and Eve ate

4. REVIEW QUESTIONS
1. Where did Adam and Eve live? **(In the Garden of Eden)**
2. What tree was in the middle of the garden? **(The Tree of the Knowledge of Good and Evil)**
3. What did God tell them about the tree? **(Not to eat the fruit from the tree)**
4. Who tricked Eve into eating the fruit? **(The serpent/Satan)**
5. How did God punish Adam and Eve? **(By making them leave the garden)**

Life Application Question: What should we do if we disobey God (sin)? **(Ask God to forgive us)**

5. PRAYER FOCUS
Forgiveness, and wisdom in making correct choices

REVIEW & MEMORY TIME

REVIEW OPTIONS:
- Overhead Game
  pg. 107, #3
- Bible Tic-Tac-Toe
  pg. 107, #4
- Bible Bingo
  pg. 107, #5
- Bible Basketball
  pg. 107, #6

MEMORY VERSE OPTIONS:
- Memory Verse Mix
  pg. 113, #2
- Memory Verse Pocket
  pg. 113, #6
- Clue Word Memory Cards
  pg. 114, #8

CAIN & ABEL

STORY REFERENCE: Genesis 4
MEMORY VERSE: Galatians 5:26 — Let us not become conceited, provoking and envying each other.

STORYTELLING TIME

1. TO THE STORYTELLER
BEFORE YOU BEGIN: Ask review questions from the previous stories.
Our society, especially the media, is continually reinforcing the idea to children (and to us) that people need to have material things to be important. With this mind-set, jealousy can creep in and make people act in ways that normally they would not. When a child sees another person who seems to have it all, or seems to get all of the attention, jealousy can easily creep in. This story should prove to children that being jealous only causes pain and that Christ doesn't want people to feel jealousy toward others.

2. STORYTELLING METHODS
A. Children As Bible Characters — pg. 67, #2
B. Storytelling Puppet — pg. 68, #8
C. SuperCards/Overhead Transparencies — pg. 70, #13

3. MEMORY OBJECT: A Shredded Wheat box
GIVEAWAY: A sugar-coated shredded wheat square
STORY/OBJECT ASSOCIATION: The grain sacrifice that Cain brought to God

4. REVIEW QUESTIONS
1. Who were the two sons in this story? **(Cain and Abel)**
2. What did Cain bring as an offering to God? **(Crops he had grown)**
3. What did Abel bring as an offering to God? **(The best sheep from his flock)**
4. Why was Cain jealous of Abel? **(Because God accepted Abel's offering, but not Cain's)**
5. What terrible thing did Cain do to Abel? **(He killed Abel.)**

LIFE APPLICATION QUESTION: What does jealousy cause people to do? **(It causes them to sin.)**

5. PRAYER FOCUS
Repentance for jealous feelings toward others

REVIEW & MEMORY TIME

REVIEW OPTIONS:
- Story Diorama
   pg. 111, #22
- Bible Story Mural
   pg. 111, #26
- Bible Story Bag
   pg. 112, #27
- Change the Bible Story
   pg. 112, #28

MEMORY VERSE OPTIONS:
- Pass the Hat
   pg. 114, #9
- Round Table Memory
   pg. 115, #14
- Memory Verse Square
   pg. 116, #17

4 NOAH'S ARK

NOAH'S ARK

STORY REFERENCE: Genesis 6
MEMORY VERSE: Genesis 6:8 — But Noah found favor in the eyes of the LORD.

STORYTELLING TIME

1. TO THE STORYTELLER
BEFORE YOU BEGIN: Ask review questions from the previous stories.
When God chose Noah to build the ark, He saw a man who would obey His commands even though Noah would be mocked and ridiculed for doing something that, in man's eyes, was foolish. Noah trusted God completely, and because he did, he found favor in God's eyes. This story shows how important it was for Noah to obey God. His obedience meant not only saving his own life, but the lives of his family members. For us today, finding favor with God means the assurance of eternal life in heaven.

2. STORYTELLING METHODS
A. Story Tape — pg. 67, #1
B. Seat Performers — pg. 68, #6
C. Bible Story Apron — pg. 69, #10

3. MEMORY OBJECT: Animal Crackers or a toy boat
GIVEAWAY: An animal cracker
STORY/OBJECT ASSOCIATION: The animals that Noah took with him onto the ark

4. REVIEW QUESTIONS
1. Why did God choose Noah to build the ark? **(Because Noah had obeyed God)**
2. Why did God want to destroy all of the people? **(Because they were wicked)**
3. What was Noah supposed to take on the ark? **(Two of every animal)**
4. Who were Noah's three sons? **(Shem, Ham, and Japheth)**
5. Why do people sometimes laugh at God? **(Because they don't love Him)**

Life Application Question: How can we find favor with God? **(By loving Him and obeying His commands)**

5. PRAYER FOCUS
Strength to obey God's commands

REVIEW & MEMORY TIME

REVIEW OPTIONS:
- Bible Bingo
  pg. 107, #5
- What Am I?
  pg. 108, #10
- Balloon Pop Review
  pg. 109, #13
- Beach Ball Review
  pg. 109, #15

MEMORY VERSE OPTIONS:
- Memory Verse Book
  pg. 113, #1
- Balloon Pop Race
  pg. 117, #21
- Name That Verse
  pg. 118, #23

TOWER OF BABEL

Story Reference: Genesis 11:1-9
Memory Verse: Proverbs 16:18 — Pride goes before destruction, a haughty spirit before a fall.

STORYTELLING TIME

1. TO THE STORYTELLER

BEFORE YOU BEGIN: Ask review questions from the previous stories.
This story proves that when we become too proud, or feel completely self-sufficient, God seems to have a way of stopping us in our tracks and letting us know that we need to get our focus back on Him. What children should learn from this story is that it is all right for a person to feel proud of his accomplishments, but when a person's motive is solely for personal gain or glory, it is sinful pride.

2. STORYTELLING METHODS
  A. Map It Out — pg. 67, #4
  B. Spray Can Storytelling — pg. 69, #9
  C. TV Story — pg. 70, #15

3. MEMORY OBJECT: Legos
  Giveaway: Sand-colored sponges cut into rectangular pieces
  Story/Object Association: The blocks the men used to build the Tower of Babel

4. REVIEW QUESTIONS
  1. When did everyone understand each other? (**In early Bible times**)
  2. What did some men decide to build? (**A city and a tower**)
  3. How tall did the men want the tower to be? (**Tall enough to reach to the sky**)
  4. Why did the men want to build the tower? (**So the people would tell them how great they were**)
  5. Why did God mix up the language? (**So the men could not understand each other and would have to stop building the tower**)

  Life Application Question: When is it wrong to be proud? (**When we forget about God and don't thank Him for the good things that happen to us**)

5. PRAYER FOCUS
  Forgiveness of sinful pride

REVIEW & MEMORY TIME

REVIEW OPTIONS:
- Give Me a Clue
  pg. 107, #2
- Name Scramble
  pg. 108, #7
- Bible Pictionary
  pg. 108, #9
- Bible Baseball
  pg. 109, #12

MEMORY VERSE OPTIONS:
- Memory Verse Mix
  pg. 113, #2
- Memory Verse Match
  pg. 114, #7
- Catch a Verse
  pg. 115, #12

MEMORY OBJECT OPTIONS:
- Bible Biography
  pg. 119, #1
- Object Sequence
  pg. 119, #5

6 SODOM & GOMORRAH

STORY REFERENCE: Genesis 19:1-29
MEMORY VERSE: 2 Corinthians 6:14a — Do not be yoked together with unbelievers. For what do righteousness and wickedness have in common?

STORYTELLING TIME

1. TO THE STORYTELLER
BEFORE YOU BEGIN: Ask review questions from the previous stories.
The cities of Sodom and Gomorrah may unfortunately remind us a lot of our world today. In very subtle ways, evil and wickedness are presented to our children each day as alternatives to godliness. For example, children are being told to accept homosexuality as just another lifestyle even though God has specifically told us in Leviticus 18:22 that it is sin. This story is a reminder of how imperative it is that our children understand and believe that it is all right to stand apart from the world and not accept its standards, but only those of God.

2. STORYTELLING METHODS
A. Storyteller As a Bible Character — pg. 67, #3
B. SuperCards/Overhead Transparencies — pg. 70, #13
C. Narration — pg. 70, #14

3. MEMORY OBJECT: A Morton's Salt container
Giveaway: A restaurant-size salt packet
Story/Object Association: How Lot's wife turned into salt

4. REVIEW QUESTIONS
1. Where did Lot live? What city was nearby? (**Sodom, Gomorrah**)
2. What were the people like who lived there? (**They were wicked.**)
3. Who did God send to Lot's house? (**Two angels**)
4. What did they tell Lot? (**To leave the city and not look back**)
5. What happened to Lot's wife? Why? (**She turned into a statue of salt because she looked back at the burning cities.**)

Life Application Question: What should we stay away from? (**Anything that would make us do something that would not please God**)

5. PRAYER FOCUS
Forgiveness of sinful pride

REVIEW & MEMORY TIME

REVIEW OPTIONS:
- Bible Tic-Tac-Toe pg. 107, #4
- Bible Bingo pg. 107, #5
- Newspaper Search pg. 110, #17
- Story Card Spinner pg. 110, #19

MEMORY VERSE OPTIONS:
- Guess a Letter pg. 115, #13
- Memory Ladder pg. 116, #16
- Memory Verse Sticks pg. 117, #20

MEMORY OBJECT OPTIONS:
- Object Match pg. 119, #2
- Object Poster pg. 120, #7

ABRAHAM OFFERS ISAAC

Story Reference: Genesis 22:1-19
Memory Verse: Genesis 22:18 — And through your offspring all nations on earth will be blessed, because you have obeyed me.

STORYTELLING TIME

1. TO THE STORYTELLER
BEFORE YOU BEGIN: Ask review questions from the previous stories.
Children are self-centered by nature. Asking them to give up a special toy or game may not always be easy for them. God wants us to give of our time, talents, and resources, so it is never too early to learn this lesson. When God asked Abraham to sacrifice his son on an altar, this was the ultimate gift that Abraham could give. Little did Abraham know that many years later God would ask the same thing of himself. When children hear this story, they should think about the gifts that they could give to God.

2. STORYTELLING METHODS
A. Story Tape — pg. 67, #1
B. Children As Bible Characters — pg. 67, #2
C. Storytelling Puppet — pg. 68, #8

3. MEMORY OBJECT: A rubber knife
Giveaway: A small plastic knife
Story/Object Association: The knife Abraham was going to use to sacrifice his son.

4. REVIEW QUESTIONS
1. Who was Abraham's son? **(Isaac)**
2. Where did Abraham travel to for the sacrifice? **(Mount Moriah)**
3. What did God tell Abraham to do with his son? **(Sacrifice him)**
4. Why did God test Abraham? **(To see if Abraham would do whatever He asked)**
5. What did God send for Abraham to sacrifice? **(A ram)**

Life Application Question: What would you give up for God? *(Allow for a variety of answers.)*

5. PRAYER FOCUS
Giving our gifts or talents for God's glory

REVIEW & MEMORY TIME

REVIEW OPTIONS:
- Give Me a Clue
  pg. 107, #2
- Bible Basketball
  pg. 107, #6
- Balloon Pop Review
  pg. 109, #13
- Card Collection
  pg. 110, #20

MEMORY VERSE OPTIONS:
- Memory Verse Envelope
  pg. 113, #3
- Clothespin Review
  pg. 113, #5
- Memory Verse Puppet
  pg. 117, #19

MEMORY OBJECT OPTIONS:
- Object Bag
  pg. 119, #3
- Musical Objects
  pg. 119, #6

8   JACOB & ESAU

JACOB AND ESAU

Story Reference: Genesis 25:19-34
Memory Verse: 1 Thessalonians 5:21 — Test everything. Hold on to the good.

STORYTELLING TIME

1. TO THE STORYTELLER
BEFORE YOU BEGIN: Ask review questions from the previous stories.
When Esau traded his birthright to Jacob for a bowl of stew, all he was thinking about was satisfying his hunger. He wasn't thinking of what he would lose in the end. As adults, we may have already learned a similar lesson and now think of long-term effects before making quick decisions. But, as you well know, children are not long-term thinkers. They live for the moment. This story can teach a valuable lesson to children. They will still make mistakes, but as they get older, they can always look back on this story and relate to Esau and the loss that he felt.

2. STORYTELLING METHODS
A. Storyteller As a Bible Character — pg. 67, #3
B. Bible Story Apron — pg. 69, #10
C. Draw a Picture — pg. 68, #7

3. MEMORY OBJECT: A can of beans or soup
Giveaway: A dried bean
Story/Object Association: The soup that Jacob offered Esau in exchange for his birthright

4. REVIEW QUESTIONS
1. Who were Isaac and Rebekah's twin sons? (**Jacob and Esau**)
2. Which son was the oldest? (**Esau**)
3. What special honor did the oldest son receive? (**A birthright**)
4. Why did Esau trade his birthright? (**He wanted a bowl of stew to eat**)
5. Why would Jacob want Esau's birthright? (**So he could be the next leader of his family and receive many of his fathers belongings**)

Life Application Question: What wouldn't you give away? Why? *(Allow for a variety of answers.)*

5. PRAYER FOCUS
Wisdom to make wise choices

REVIEW & MEMORY TIME

REVIEW OPTIONS:
- Overhead Game
  pg. 107, #3
- Guess My Name
  pg. 109, #11
- Who Am I?
  pg. 110, #16
- Story Review Cards
  pg. 111, #23

MEMORY VERSE OPTIONS:
- Chalkboard Verse
  pg. 114, #10
- Memory Balloon-a-Thon
  pg. 115, #11
- Memory Choir
  pg. 115, #15

MEMORY OBJECT OPTIONS:
- Name That Object
  pg. 119, #4
- Memory Object Bookmark
  pg. 120, #9

JACOB WRESTLES WITH GOD 9

STORY REFERENCE: Genesis 32:22-32
MEMORY VERSE: Genesis 32:28 — Then the man said, "Your name will no longer be Jacob, but Israel, because you have struggled with God and with men and have overcome."

STORYTELLING TIME

1. TO THE STORYTELLER
BEFORE YOU BEGIN: Ask review questions from the previous stories.
The Israelite people in the Old Testament knew what it meant to have a blessing from God. Many times, a blessing meant protection and prosperity. It was something they didn't take lightly. Anything good that happened, they knew, came from God. Our world tries to tell us that whatever good comes our way is by pure luck, or because we worked hard enough to earn the reward. With this story, you can show that when we work to serve God, He will want to send blessings our way. And when He does, we need to remember that they came from Him.

2. STORYTELLING METHODS
A. Story Tape — pg. 67, #1
B. Bible Story Cards — pg. 69, #11
C. Bible Time Machine — pg. 69, #12

3. MEMORY OBJECT: A name tag
GIVEAWAY: A name tag for each child. If possible, ahead of time write the meaning of each child's name on his name tag.
STORY/OBJECT ASSOCIATION: When God changed Jacob's name to Israel

4. REVIEW QUESTIONS
1. Who was Jacob traveling home to meet? **(His brother, Esau)**
2. What did Jacob and God do? **(They wrestled.)**
3. What did Jacob want from God? **(A blessing)**
4. Why was God pleased with Jacob? **(Because Jacob wanted a blessing badly enough to fight for it)**
5. What new name did God give to Jacob? **(Israel)**
LIFE APPLICATION QUESTION: How has God blessed you? *(By giving me family, food, shelter — allow for a variety of answers.)*

5. PRAYER FOCUS
Thankfulness to God for His many blessings

REVIEW & MEMORY TIME

REVIEW OPTIONS:
- Character Quotes
  pg. 108, #8
- Guess My Name
  pg. 109, #11
- Beach Ball Review
  pg. 109, #15
- Bible Story Bag
  pg. 112, #27

MEMORY VERSE OPTIONS:
- Memory Verse Golf
  pg. 116, #18
- Memory Verse Mobile
  pg. 117, #22
- Memory Verse Bulletin Board
  pg. 118, #24

MEMORY OBJECT OPTIONS:
- Object Match
  pg. 119, #2
- Object Mural
  pg. 120, #8

10 JOSEPH'S COAT

JOSEPH'S COAT

STORY REFERENCE: Genesis 37
MEMORY VERSE: Ephesians 4:32a — Be kind and compassionate to one another.

STORYTELLING TIME

1. TO THE STORYTELLER
BEFORE YOU BEGIN: Ask review questions from the previous stories.
As in the story of Cain and Abel, jealousy also tore Jacob's family apart. Jealousy has continued through many generations. Joseph's brothers were jealous of him. Part of the responsibility for this might have been Jacob's for "playing favorites" by giving his favorite son that fancy coat. Nevertheless, Joseph's brothers' jealousy was still wrong. Life isn't always fair. Children can become jealous when others get better grades, get more attention, or have nicer things. This is a great story for teaching children how important it is to avoid becoming jealous at all costs! It cost this family too much.

2. STORYTELLING METHODS
A. Children As Bible Characters — pg. 67, #2
B. Spray Can Storytelling — pg. 69, #9
C. TV Story — pg. 70, #15

3. MEMORY OBJECT: A brightly colored coat/robe or swatch of cloth
GIVEAWAY: A piece of brightly colored cloth
STORY/OBJECT ASSOCIATION: The robe that Joseph received from his father, Jacob

4. REVIEW QUESTIONS
1. Who was Jacob's favorite son? (**Joseph**)
2. What special gift did Jacob make for his son? (**A coat**)
3. Why were Joseph's brothers jealous of him? (**Because their father loved Joseph more than he loved them**)
4. How did Joseph's brothers get rid of him? (**They sold him to slave traders.**)
5. What did Jacob think happened to Joseph? (**An animal killed him.**)

LIFE APPLICATION QUESTION: How have you hurt someone? (**By talking mean, hitting someone** — *allow for a variety of answers.*)

5. PRAYER FOCUS
Forgiveness for hurting others

REVIEW & MEMORY TIME

REVIEW OPTIONS:
■ Bible Bingo
   pg. 107, #5
■ Bible Baseball
   pg. 109, #12
■ Shaving Cream Review
   pg. 110, #18
■ Bible Time Capsule
   pg. 110, #21

MEMORY VERSE OPTIONS:
■ Memory Verse Mix
   pg. 113, #2
■ Clothespin Review
   pg. 113, #5
■ Catch a Verse
   pg. 115, #12

MEMORY OBJECT OPTIONS:
■ Bible Biography
   pg. 119, #1
■ Object Sequence
   pg. 119, #5

JOSEPH IN PRISON

JOSEPH IN PRISON

Story Reference: Genesis 39 – 40
Memory Verse: Genesis 39:20b-21a — But while Joseph was there in the prison, the LORD was with him.

STORYTELLING TIME

1. TO THE STORYTELLER
BEFORE YOU BEGIN: Ask review questions from the previous ten stories.
No one likes to be accused of something he didn't do, especially a child. And you can be sure that a child will let you know if he has been wrongfully accused. Children need to come away from this story knowing that, like Joseph, at some time they will be wrongfully hurt by others — verbally or maybe even physically. When this happens, they should remember that God loves each of them and will be with them just like He was with Joseph.

2. STORYTELLING METHODS
A. Story Tape — pg. 67, #1
B. Storytelling Puppet — pg. 68, #8
C. SuperCards/Overhead Transparencies — pg. 70, #13

3. MEMORY OBJECT: A key
Giveaway: A small key
Story/Object Association: Joseph locked up in a prison cell

4. REVIEW QUESTIONS
1. Why was Joseph put into prison? (**Because he was accused of a crime, though he did not do it**)
2. Who put Joseph in charge of the prisoners? (**The warden**)
3. What two servants did Pharaoh send to prison? (**The baker and cupbearer**)
4. What did Joseph do for these servants? (**He interpreted their dreams.**)
5. What did Joseph ask the cupbearer to do? (**To ask Pharaoh if he would free Joseph from prison**)

Life Application Question: How have you been blamed by mistake? (*Accept reasonable answers.*)

5. PRAYER FOCUS
Forgiveness of others

REVIEW & MEMORY TIME

REVIEW OPTIONS:
- Card Scramble
  pg. 107, #1
- Bible Pictionary
  pg. 108, #9
- Story Review Cards
  pg. 111, #23
- Bible Story Mural
  pg. 111, #26

MEMORY VERSE OPTIONS:
- Round Table Memory
  pg. 115, #14
- Memory Verse Golf
  pg. 116, #18
- Memory Verse Puppet
  pg. 117, #19

MEMORY OBJECT OPTIONS:
- Object Bag
  pg. 119, #3
- Object Poster
  pg. 120, #7

25

12 JOSEPH RULES IN EGYPT

Story Reference: Genesis 41 – 42
Memory Verse: Romans 8:28 — And we know that in all things God works for the good of those who love him, who have been called according to his purpose.

STORYTELLING TIME

1. TO THE STORYTELLER
BEFORE YOU BEGIN: Ask review questions from the previous ten stories. Many times, a person is not able to figure out or fully understand God's faithfulness until he is older and can look back at his life and see how God has carried him through many different circumstances. This story is a wonderful example for all of us. Make this a story that children can go back to and remember that, like Joseph, even in their toughest times they should never turn from God. They may never find out what wonderful things God has waiting for them around the corner.

2. STORYTELLING METHODS
A. Map It Out — pg. 67, #4
B. Draw a Picture — pg. 68, #7
C. Narration — pg. 70, #14

3. MEMORY OBJECT: An oatmeal container
Giveaway: A small bag of oatmeal
Story/Object Association: The grain that was stored for the famine

4. REVIEW QUESTIONS
1. What happened in Pharaoh's dream? **(Seven thin cows ate seven fat cows.)**
2. What servant remembered Joseph from prison? **(The cupbearer)**
3. Who interpreted Pharaoh's dream? **(Joseph)**
4. What did Pharaoh's dream mean? **(That Egypt would have seven good years for raising crops and then seven years of famine)**
5. What was Joseph's job when he became a ruler? **(He was to make sure that there was enough food stored for the seven-year famine.)**

Life Application Question: How is God faithful to you? **(He protects me, gives me food —** *allow for a variety of answers.***)**

5. PRAYER FOCUS
Thankfulness for God's faithfulness

REVIEW & MEMORY TIME

REVIEW OPTIONS:
■ Bible Basketball
  pg. 107, #6
■ Character Quotes
  pg. 108, #8
■ Card Collection
  pg. 110, #20
■ Change the Bible Story
  pg. 112, #28

MEMORY VERSE OPTIONS:
■ Memory Verse Envelope
  pg. 113, #3
■ Memory Verse Match
  pg. 114, #7
■ Pass the Hat
  pg. 114, #9

MEMORY OBJECT OPTIONS:
■ Musical Objects
  pg. 119, #6
■ Object Mural
  pg. 120, #8

BABY MOSES

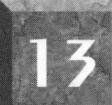

STORY REFERENCE: Exodus 2:1-10
MEMORY VERSE: Psalm 91:2 — I will say of the LORD, "He is my refuge and my fortress, my God, in whom I trust."

STORYTELLING TIME

1. TO THE STORYTELLER

BEFORE YOU BEGIN: Ask review questions from the previous ten stories.
We all have a desire to be protected because we need to feel "safe." Parents have a special responsibility to make their children feel safe. Imagine the emotional anguish that Moses' mother must have felt by giving up that cherished responsibility. She literally had to put her son in God's protection. What faith! What a powerful story showing God's love and protection for His children, even a little baby! Because of the love and trust that this mother had, God used her son to do mighty things for His kingdom.

2. STORYTELLING METHODS
   A. Storyteller As a Bible Character — pg. 67, #3
   B. Floor Map — pg. 68, #5
   C. TV Story — pg. 70, #15

3. MEMORY OBJECT: A doll, basket, or cattail
   Giveaway: A small, plastic baby doll
   Story/Object Association: Baby Moses

4. REVIEW QUESTIONS
   1. Who did Pharaoh order to be killed? Why? **(Hebrew baby boys; because he thought there were too many Hebrews in his land)**
   2. What did Moses' mother do to save him? **(She put him into a basket and placed it in the river.)**
   3. Did Moses' mother have faith in God? How? **(Yes; by believing that God would protect her baby while he was in the river)**
   4. Who watched the basket float in the river? **(Miriam, Moses' sister)**
   5. Who found Moses in the basket? **(Pharaoh's daughter)**

   Life Application Question: How has God protected you from harm? *(Children will have many stories.)*

5. PRAYER FOCUS
   Thankfulness for God's protection

REVIEW & MEMORY TIME

REVIEW OPTIONS:
- Name Scramble
  pg. 108, #7
- What Am I?
  pg. 108, #10
- Guess My Name
  pg. 109, #11
- Story Diorama
  pg. 111, #22

MEMORY VERSE OPTIONS:
- Memory Choir
  pg. 115, #15
- Memory Verse Sticks
  pg. 117, #20
- Name That Verse
  pg. 118, #23

MEMORY OBJECT OPTIONS:
- Name That Object
  pg. 119, #4
- Memory Object Bookmark
  pg. 120, #9

14 THE BURNING BUSH

Story Reference: Exodus 3
Memory Verse: Exodus 3:2 — There the angel of the Lord appeared to him in flames of fire from within a bush. Moses saw that though the bush was on fire it did not burn up.

STORYTELLING TIME

1. TO THE STORYTELLER
BEFORE YOU BEGIN: Ask review questions from the previous ten stories.
Most people cannot say that they have audibly heard God's voice speak to them. For most of us, God speaks through our conscience, through the Scriptures, through other people and through prayer. The most important lesson that a child should learn from this story is that however God speaks to us, we need to listen and obey. What an honor and privilege to know that God wants to speak with us so that we can have a personal relationship with Him!

2. STORYTELLING METHODS
A. Story Tape — pg. 67, #1
B. Storyteller As a Bible Character — pg. 67, #3
C. Narration — pg. 70, #14

3. MEMORY OBJECT: A small bush or plant
Giveaway: A branch from a bush
Story/Object Association: The burning bush

4. REVIEW QUESTIONS
1. Where did Moses move to after he grew up? (**Midian**)
2. What was different about the bush Moses saw? (**The bush was on fire, but it didn't burn.**)
3. What was Moses supposed to tell Pharaoh? (**To free the Israelites**)
4. How did Moses feel when God spoke to him? (**Afraid**)
5. Why did God say Moses should not be afraid? (**Because God would be with him**)

Life Application Question: How does God speak to us today? (**Through our conscience, through the Scriptures, through other people and through prayer**)

5. PRAYER FOCUS
Praise to God for the ability to have a personal relationship with Him

REVIEW & MEMORY TIME

REVIEW OPTIONS:
- Give Me a Clue
  pg. 107, #2
- Bible Basketball
  pg. 107, #6
- Balloon Pop Review
  pg. 109, #13
- Story Card Spinner
  pg. 110, #19

MEMORY VERSE OPTIONS:
- Memory Verse Card Drill
  pg. 113, #4
- Clue Word Memory Cards
  pg. 114, #8
- Chalkboard Verse
  pg. 114, #10

MEMORY OBJECT OPTIONS:
- Bible Biography
  pg. 119, #1
- Memory Object Bookmark
  pg. 120, #9

THE PLAGUES

Story Reference: Exodus 7 – 10
Memory Verse: Jeremiah 33:3 — Call to me and I will answer you and tell you great and unsearchable things you do not know.

STORYTELLING TIME

1. TO THE STORYTELLER
BEFORE YOU BEGIN: Ask review questions from the previous ten stories.
The Israelites prayed for God to free them from Egyptian slavery. He answered their prayers, but probably not as quickly as they would have liked. Use this story to show children that God does answer the prayers of His people. As children's leaders, we must first teach children how to pray. Then, we need to show them how God has answered prayers in the past, how He answers prayers today, and why He will answer our prayers in the future.

2. STORYTELLING METHODS
A. Seat Performers — pg. 68, #6
B. Bible Story Apron — pg. 69, #10
C. TV Story — pg. 70, #15

3. MEMORY OBJECT: A frog (plastic or real)
Giveaway: A frog sticker
Story/Object Association: One of the plagues that God sent to Egypt

4. REVIEW QUESTIONS
1. Who wanted God to free them from slavery? **(The Israelites)**
2. Who did God send to talk to Pharaoh? **(Moses and Aaron)**
3. What did they tell Pharaoh? **(To free the Israelites)**
4. What happened each time Pharaoh said, "No"? **(God sent a plague to Egypt.)**
5. What were the plagues that God sent to Egypt? **(The waters turned to blood; frogs; gnats; flies; the death of livestock; boils; deadly hail; locusts; and complete darkness)**

Life Application Question: How does God answer us when we pray? **(Through His Word/the Bible, other people, and by guiding us through the Holy Spirit)**

5. PRAYER FOCUS
Thankfulness to God for answered prayers

REVIEW & MEMORY TIME

REVIEW OPTIONS:
- Overhead Game
  pg. 107, #3
- Bible Basketball
  pg. 107, #6
- Newspaper Search
  pg. 110, #17
- Card Collection
  pg. 110, #20

MEMORY VERSE OPTIONS:
- Memory Ladder
  pg. 116, #16
- Balloon Pop Race
  pg. 117, #21
- Memory Verse Bulletin Board
  pg. 118, #24

MEMORY OBJECT OPTIONS:
- Object Match
  pg. 119, #2
- Object Sequence
  pg. 119, #5

16 THE FIRST PASSOVER

Story Reference: Exodus 11:1 – 12:31
Memory Verse: 1 John 1:7b — And the blood of Jesus, his Son, purifies us from all sin.

STORYTELLING TIME

1. TO THE STORYTELLER
BEFORE YOU BEGIN: Ask review questions from the previous ten stories.
This is one of the most powerful stories in the Old Testament and contains one of the most important lessons that we **must** teach our children. The instructions that God gave to the Israelites for the first Passover were very important and quite clear. He provided a way for the Israelites to save their sons from death. This story clearly shows that God has given us, like the Israelites, instructions through His Word. He has provided a way for us, if we follow these instructions, to be saved from eternal death.

2. STORYTELLING METHODS
A. Draw a Picture — pg. 68, #7
B. Storytelling Puppet — pg. 68, #8
C. Bible Time Machine — pg. 69, #12

3. MEMORY OBJECT: A toy lamb or bag of cotton balls
Giveaway: A white cotton ball
Story/Object Association: The lambs were sacrificed so the oldest sons could live.

4. REVIEW QUESTIONS
1. What was the last plague God sent to Egypt? (**Death of firstborn sons**)
2. When did God say He would pass over Egypt? (**Around midnight**)
3. What instructions did God give to the Israelites? (**Each family was to sacrifice a lamb or a goat, take the blood, and put it on the top and sides of their doorframe.**)
4. What happened to Pharaoh's firstborn son? (**He was killed.**)
5. Why was that night called the "Passover"? (**Because God passed over the homes of the Israelites who obeyed His instructions, and their firstborn sons were not killed.**)

Life Application Question: Why is it important to follow instructions? (**Because they can help us to do what is right.**)

5. PRAYER FOCUS
Asking for help to follow God's instructions

REVIEW & MEMORY TIME

REVIEW OPTIONS:
- Card Scramble
  pg. 107, #1
- Bible Tic-Tac-Toe
  pg. 107, #4
- Bible Bingo
  pg. 107, #5
- Bible Charades
  pg. 109, #14

MEMORY VERSE OPTIONS:
- Memory Verse Pocket
  pg. 113, #6
- Memory Balloon-a-Thon
  pg. 115, #11
- Memory Verse Square
  pg. 116, #17

MEMORY OBJECT OPTIONS:
- Object Bag
  pg. 119, #3
- Object Poster
  pg. 120, #7

CROSSING THE RED SEA

STORY REFERENCE: Exodus 13 – 14
MEMORY VERSE: Exodus 14:14 — The LORD will fight for you; you need only to be still.

STORYTELLING TIME

1. TO THE STORYTELLER
BEFORE YOU BEGIN: Ask review questions from the previous ten stories.
Pulling a quarter out from behind someone's ear is a common trick that most people have seen. Many people know the secret to this trick, so it isn't very fascinating. The parting of the Red Sea is a miracle that humans cannot explain and that will always intrigue people. God's miracles today may not always seem as exciting as the parting of the Red Sea, but the miracles that do happen — the healing of sick people, answered prayers, and even the sunrise in the morning — are reminders of God's infinite power.

CROSSING THE RED SEA

2. STORYTELLING METHODS
A. Children As Bible Characters — pg. 67, #2
B. Floor Map — pg. 68, #5
C. Spray Can Storytelling — pg. 69, #9

3. MEMORY OBJECT: A large stick or staff
GIVEAWAY: A short piece of a dowel rod
STORY/OBJECT ASSOCIATION: The staff that Moses held over the water when God parted the Red Sea

4. REVIEW QUESTIONS
1. Why did Pharaoh want the Israelites back? **(He had lost his workers.)**
2. Who led the Israelites out of Egypt? **(Moses)**
3. What sea did the Israelites need to cross? **(The Red Sea)**
4. What did Moses do to make the water roll back? **(He raised his staff and stretched out his hand over the water.)**
5. What happened to the Egyptians who followed? **(They drowned.)**

LIFE APPLICATION QUESTION: Does God still perform miracles? Why? **(Yes; to show He is God)**

5. PRAYER FOCUS
Thankfulness for God's miracles, even the small ones

REVIEW & MEMORY TIME

REVIEW OPTIONS:
- Bible Basketball
  pg. 107, #6
- Name Scramble
  pg. 108, #7
- Bible Story Map
  pg. 111, #24
- Change the Bible Story
  pg. 112, #28

MEMORY VERSE OPTIONS:
- Memory Verse Mix
  pg. 113, #2
- Guess a Letter
  pg. 115, #13
- Memory Verse Mobile
  pg. 117, #22

MEMORY OBJECT OPTIONS:
- Musical Objects
  pg. 119, #6
- Memory Object Bookmark
  pg. 120, #9

18 EATING MANNA

STORY REFERENCE: Exodus 16
MEMORY VERSE: John 6:33 — For the bread of God is he who comes down from heaven and gives life to the world.

STORYTELLING TIME

1. TO THE STORYTELLER
BEFORE YOU BEGIN: Ask review questions from the previous ten stories.
In our selfish nature, we many times do not stop to think of how God is constantly providing for us. God provided for the Israelites' basic needs in many miraculous ways. This is a wonderful story for showing children that everything we have comes from God. He may not rain down bread from heaven, but He uses parents and family members to provide the things children need, like shelter, food, water, and clothing. He is our constant provider.

2. STORYTELLING METHODS
A. Bible Story Apron — pg. 69, #10
B. Bible Story Cards — pg. 69, #11
C. Bible Time Machine — pg. 69, #12

3. MEMORY OBJECT: Necco Wafers or other cookies
Giveaway: A Necco Wafer
Story/Object Association: The manna that God provided for the Israelites

4. REVIEW QUESTIONS
1. Why were the Israelites complaining to Moses? **(Because they wanted food to eat)**
2. Why did they wish they had stayed in Egypt? **(Because they had plenty of food to eat in Egypt)**
3. What did God send for the Israelites to eat? **(Manna)**
4. How much were the Israelites told to gather? **(Only enough for each day)**
5. What happened to the extra manna? **(It spoiled)**

Life Application Question: What has God provided for you? **(Food, shelter, clothing** — *allow for a variety of answers.***)**

5. PRAYER FOCUS
Thankfulness for God's provision

REVIEW & MEMORY TIME

REVIEW OPTIONS:
- Character Quotes pg. 108, #8
- Balloon Pop Review pg. 109, #13
- Bible Charades pg. 109, #14
- Bible Story Bag pg. 112, #27

MEMORY VERSE OPTIONS:
- Catch a Verse pg. 115, #12
- Memory Choir pg. 115, #15
- Memory Verse Puppet pg. 117, #19

MEMORY OBJECT OPTIONS:
- Name That Object pg. 119, #4
- Object Sequence pg. 119, #5

MOSES STRIKES THE ROCK 

STORY REFERENCE: Exodus 17:1-7
MEMORY VERSE: Philippians 2:14 — Do everything without complaining or arguing.

STORYTELLING TIME

1. TO THE STORYTELLER
BEFORE YOU BEGIN: Ask review questions from the previous ten stories. Complaining — it is one of the most time-consuming, yet useless and unproductive, things that people do. Complaining never solves the problem; it creates frustration, and nothing positive ever comes from it. So why do people do it? Because it's easy to do. This story can show children that the people in Old Testament times were not much different than people today. Help children to understand that the way to deal with problems and difficulties is not by complaining, but through prayer.

2. STORYTELLING METHODS
A. Storyteller As a Bible Character — pg. 67, #3
B. Floor Map — pg. 68, #5
C. SuperCards/Overhead Transparencies — pg. 70, #13

3. MEMORY OBJECT: A water bottle
GIVEAWAY: A small rock
Story/Object Association: The rock that Moses struck to get water for the Israelites

4. REVIEW QUESTIONS
1. Why were the Israelites angry? **(Because they didn't have any water to drink)**
2. What was Moses afraid the people would do? **(Kill him)**
3. What did God tell Moses to take with him? **(His walking stick and some of the older leaders)**
4. Where did God say He would be standing? **(In front of Moses by a rock)**
5. How did Moses get water for the Israelites? **(He hit the rock.)**

Life Application Question: What do we sometimes complain about? **(Homework, cleaning, our rooms, other people)**

5. PRAYER FOCUS
Forgiveness for complaining

REVIEW & MEMORY TIME

REVIEW OPTIONS:
- Card Scramble
  pg. 107, #1
- Bible Bingo
  pg. 107, #5
- Bible Baseball
  pg. 109, #12
- Who Am I?
  pg. 110, #16

MEMORY VERSE OPTIONS:
- Memory Verse Card Drill
  pg. 113, #4
- Pass the Hat
  pg. 114, #9
- Balloon Pop Race
  pg. 117, #21

MEMORY OBJECT OPTIONS:
- Bible Biography
  pg. 119, #1
- Object Bag
  pg. 119, #3

20 THE TEN COMMANDMENTS

STORY REFERENCE: Exodus 20
MEMORY VERSE: Deuteronomy 6:17a — Be sure to keep the commands of the LORD your God.

STORYTELLING TIME

1. TO THE STORYTELLER
BEFORE YOU BEGIN: Ask review questions from the previous ten stories.
When you hear the word "rules," what comes to your mind? Do you think of children, school, church, grandma's house, or maybe even breaking rules? Children many times will see rules as something limiting rather than freeing. Use this story to help children see that God's rules, or commandments, were given out of love to help His children to understand what is right and wrong. They were also given to protect us. As God's children, He only wants what is best for us.

2. STORYTELLING METHODS
A. Draw a Picture — pg. 68, #7
B. Storytelling Puppet — pg. 68, #8
C. Narration — pg. 70, #14

3. MEMORY OBJECT: A scroll
GIVEAWAY: A scroll with the Ten Commandments written on it (see page 131)
STORY/OBJECT ASSOCIATION: The rules that God has given to us

4. REVIEW QUESTIONS
1. What mountain did Moses climb? **(Mount Sinai)**
2. How many rules did God give to Moses? **(Ten)**
3. What are these rules called? **(The Ten Commandments)**
4. What did God write the rules on? **(Stone tablets)**
5. How many rules can you remember? *(Have the children list the rules.)*

Life Application Question: Why did God give us rules? **(To let us know what He expects of us, to help and protect us)**

5. PRAYER FOCUS
Help in following God's rules for us

REVIEW & MEMORY TIME

REVIEW OPTIONS:
- Give Me a Clue pg. 107, #2
- Bible Basketball pg. 107, #6
- Name Scramble pg. 108, #7
- Bible Time Capsule pg. 110, #21

MEMORY VERSE OPTIONS:
- Clue Word Memory Cards pg. 114, #8
- Chalkboard Verse pg. 114, #10
- Name That Verse pg. 118, #23

MEMORY OBJECT OPTIONS:
- Object Match pg. 119, #2
- Object Mural pg. 120, #8

THE GOLDEN CALF

21

STORY REFERENCE: Exodus 32
MEMORY VERSE: Exodus 20:3 — You shall have no other gods before me.

STORYTELLING TIME

1. TO THE STORYTELLER

BEFORE YOU BEGIN: Ask review questions from the previous ten stories. This story not only reinforces why we should serve God only, but also brings in a factor on which we, as children's workers, need to focus our attention — worship! One of the most important things we will do as we minister to children is to show them *how to* worship. Prayer, Scripture reading, and singing Christian songs are just three different ways that we can show our love to Him. Through our actions, we show God that He is worthy of our praise. When children understand worship, they will be more willing and able participate in worship.

2. STORYTELLING METHODS

A. Story Tape — pg. 67, #1
B. Bible Story Apron — pg. 69, #10
C. TV Story — pg. 70, #15

3. MEMORY OBJECT: A bracelet or toy cow

GIVEAWAY: A friendship bracelet

STORY/OBJECT ASSOCIATION: The gold jewelry the Israelites gave to Aaron so he could make the golden calf

4. REVIEW QUESTIONS

1. Who did Moses put in charge of the Israelites? (**Aaron**)
2. Why did the Israelites want a golden idol? (**Because they wanted to worship a god that they could see**)
3. What did the people thank the golden calf for? (**For leading them out of Egypt**)
4. How did the Israelites disobey God? (**They didn't worship Him.**)
5. How did Moses react to the golden calf? (**He was angry and threw the stone tablets with the Ten Commandments onto the ground.**)

LIFE APPLICATION QUESTION: Why should we worship only God? (**Because this is the first commandment that God gave to us.**)

5. PRAYER FOCUS

Desire for praising and worshiping God only

REVIEW & MEMORY TIME

REVIEW OPTIONS:
- What Am I?
  pg. 108, #10
- Bible Baseball
  pg. 109, #12
- Card Collection
  pg. 110, #20
- Bible Story Mural
  pg. 111, #26

MEMORY VERSE OPTIONS:
- Guess a Letter
  pg. 115, #13
- Memory Verse Square
  pg. 116, #17
- Memory Verse Sticks
  pg. 117, #20

MEMORY OBJECT OPTIONS:
- Name That Object
  pg. 119, #4
- Musical Objects
  pg. 119, #6

22 THE TABERNACLE

STORY REFERENCE: Exodus 35:30 – 37:9
MEMORY VERSE: Exodus 25:8 — Then have them make a sanctuary for me, and I will dwell among them.

STORYTELLING TIME

1. TO THE STORYTELLER
BEFORE YOU BEGIN: Ask review questions from the previous ten stories.
Many times parents have trouble explaining to kids, especially teenagers, why it is important to attend church. This is a wonderful story for showing not only children, but also teenagers and adults, that God wants us to have a place where many believers can gather to worship Him. God knows how important it is for people to gather together for fellowship, not only with each other, but also with Him.

2. STORYTELLING METHODS
A. Spray Can Storytelling — pg. 69, #9
B. SuperCards/Overhead Transparencies — pg. 70, #13
C. Narration — pg. 70, #14

3. MEMORY OBJECT: A piece of canvas-colored cloth
Giveaway: A small piece of canvas-colored cloth
Story/Object Association: The material used in making the Tabernacle

4. REVIEW QUESTIONS
1. What did God tell the Israelites to build? (**The Tabernacle**)
2. Why did the Israelites go to the Tabernacle? (**To worship God**)
3. What were the names of the two special rooms? (**The Holy Place and the Most Holy Place**)
4. What hung between the two rooms? (**A curtain**)
5. Where was the ark of the covenant? (**In the Most Holy Place**)

Life Application Question: Why do we go to church? (**To worship God**)

5. PRAYER FOCUS
Thankfulness for a church to go to where we can worship God

REVIEW & MEMORY TIME

REVIEW OPTIONS:
- Guess My Name pg. 109, #11
- Balloon Pop Review pg. 109, #13
- Newspaper Search pg. 110, #17
- Tabernacle Model pg. 112, #29

MEMORY VERSE OPTIONS:
- Memory Verse Pocket pg. 113, #6
- Round Table Memory pg. 115, #14
- Memory Verse Bulletin Board pg. 118, #24

MEMORY OBJECT OPTIONS:
- Object Bag pg. 119, #3
- Object Poster pg. 120, #7

TWELVE SPIES

23

STORY REFERENCE: Numbers 13
MEMORY VERSE: Psalm 56:3 — When I am afraid, I will trust in you.

STORYTELLING TIME

1. TO THE STORYTELLER

BEFORE YOU BEGIN: Ask review questions from the previous ten stories. Children are dealing with many fears in today's world — more than we did when we were their age. Because of this, we need to show them how to deal with their fears. With this story, you can show that God understands that we may have fears, but like Joshua and Caleb, we need to trust God to help us overcome them. God always protected the Israelites when they obeyed and trusted Him, and He will do the same for each of us.

2. STORYTELLING METHODS
   A. Children As Bible Characters — pg. 67, #2
   B. Floor Map — pg. 68, #5
   C. TV Story — pg. 70, #15

3. MEMORY OBJECT: Grapes or Fig Newtons
   GIVEAWAY: Grapes
   STORY/OBJECT ASSOCIATION: The abundance of fruit the spies brought back from Canaan

4. REVIEW QUESTIONS
   1. How many spies did Moses send into Canaan? **(Twelve)**
   2. What were the spies supposed to do in Canaan? **(They were to see what the people and towns were like and what foods were grown there.)**
   3. How many days did the spies explore the land? **(Forty days)**
   4. What did the spies carry back from Canaan? **(A large cluster of grapes, pomegranates, and figs)**
   5. What report did the spies bring back to Moses? **(Ten of the spies said that the people were too large to fight, but Joshua and Caleb wanted to take the land.)**

   LIFE APPLICATION QUESTION: What makes us afraid? *(Allow for a variety of answers.)*

5. PRAYER FOCUS
   Strength when we are afraid

REVIEW & MEMORY TIME

REVIEW OPTIONS:
- Beach Ball Review
  pg. 109, #15
- Story Card Spinner
  pg. 110, #19
- Bible Story Map
  pg. 111, #24
- Bible Story Bag
  pg. 112, #27

MEMORY VERSE OPTIONS:
- Clothespin Review
  pg. 113, #5
- Memory Verse Golf
  pg. 116, #18
- Memory Verse Mobile
  pg. 117, #22

MEMORY OBJECT OPTIONS:
- Object Match
  pg. 119, #2
- Object Sequence
  pg. 119, #5

24 THE BRONZE SNAKE

STORY REFERENCE: Numbers 21:4-9
MEMORY VERSE: Proverbs 3:5 — Trust in the LORD with all your heart and lean not on your own understanding.

STORYTELLING TIME

1. TO THE STORYTELLER
BEFORE YOU BEGIN: Ask review questions from the previous ten stories.
The Israelites were constantly complaining because they were only thinking about what they didn't have instead of what they did have. Isn't that a lot like people today? When our focus is not on God, and earthly things become primary, He will use certain people or situations to get back our attention. Use this story to illustrate that God wants us to always have our attention on Him and to trust Him for what we need.

2. STORYTELLING METHODS
A. Seat Performers — pg. 68, #6
B. Draw a Picture — pg. 68, #7
C. Bible Time Machine — pg. 69, #12

3. MEMORY OBJECT: A toy snake
Giveaway: A Gummy Worm
Story/Object Association: The poisonous snakes that God sent into the Israelites' camp

4. REVIEW QUESTIONS
1. Why did the Israelites wander in the desert? **(Because they believed the bad report from the ten spies, and God did not let them enter the Promised Land.)**
2. Why were the Israelites complaining? **(Because they could not enter Canaan)**
3. How did God punish the Israelites? **(He sent poisonous snakes to their camp.)**
4. What did God tell Moses to make? **(A bronze snake to hang on a pole)**
5. How did God use this to help the Israelites? **(He would heal anyone who had been bitten by a snake if the person would look up at the bronze snake.)**

Life Application Question: Why do people complain instead of trust God?
(Because they don't like to wait for God to help them)

5. PRAYER FOCUS
Help in trusting God instead of complaining

REVIEW & MEMORY TIME

REVIEW OPTIONS:
- Give Me a Clue pg. 107, #2
- Bible Charades pg. 109, #14
- Story Diorama pg. 111, #22
- Change the Bible Story pg. 112, #28

MEMORY VERSE OPTIONS:
- Memory Verse Envelope pg. 113, #3
- Memory Verse Match pg. 114, #7
- Memory Ladder pg. 116, #16

MEMORY OBJECT OPTIONS:
- Name That Object pg. 119, #4
- Memory Object Bookmark pg. 120, #9

BALAAM'S DONKEY   25

Story Reference: Numbers 22
Memory Verse: Hebrews 3:15 — Today, if you hear his voice, do not harden your hearts as you did in the rebellion.

STORYTELLING TIME

1. TO THE STORYTELLER
BEFORE YOU BEGIN: Ask review questions from the previous ten stories.
It is very easy to find yourself just going through the motions of life and giving God a back seat in our minds. Then, a crisis comes without warning. The life application question for this story is "How does God get your attention?" This story can teach children in a powerful way that if we are constantly in touch with God through prayer and reading the Scriptures, God will have our attention. It's when we stray and don't have our eyes on Him that He finds ways to get our focus back on Him.

2. STORYTELLING METHODS
A. Story Tape — pg. 67, #1
B. Storyteller As a Bible Character — pg. 67, #3
C. SuperCards/Overhead Transparencies — pg. 70, #13

3. MEMORY OBJECT: A toy donkey
Giveaway: A toy donkey
Story/Object Association: Balaam's donkey

4. REVIEW QUESTIONS
1. Who did the king think would attack Moab? (**The Israelites**)
2. Who did the king send to talk to Balaam? (**The king's messengers**)
3. What did the king want Balaam to do? (**Put a curse on the Israelites**)
4. What did the king offer to give Balaam? (**Money**)
5. How did God get Balaam's attention? (**He made Balaam's donkey talk.**)

Life Application Question: How does God get your attention? *(Allow for a variety of answers.)*

5. PRAYER FOCUS
Listening to God

REVIEW & MEMORY TIME

REVIEW OPTIONS:
- Overhead Game
  pg. 107, #3
- Bible Basketball
  pg. 107, #6
- Balloon Pop Review
  pg. 109, #13
- Story Card Spinner
  pg. 110, #19

MEMORY VERSE OPTIONS:
- Memory Verse Book
  pg. 113, #1
- Pass the Hat
  pg. 114, #9
- Balloon Pop Race
  pg. 117, #21

MEMORY OBJECT OPTIONS:
- Bible Biography
  pg. 119, #1
- Musical Objects
  pg. 119, #6

26 CROSSING THE JORDAN

STORY REFERENCE: Joshua 3 – 4
MEMORY VERSE: Hebrews 10:23 — Let us hold unswervingly to the hope we profess, for he who promised is faithful.

STORYTELLING TIME

1. TO THE STORYTELLER
BEFORE YOU BEGIN: Ask review questions from the previous ten stories.
In homes where promises made to children are consistently broken, a child can only wonder when a promise that has been made will truly be kept. Is it such a surprise that children have a hard time trusting? This Bible story can be an example to children of how God kept His promises to the Israelites. What a joy to know that as Christians we can look to Scripture and see how God kept His promises in the past and can have the assurance that He will keep His promises in the future.

2. STORYTELLING METHODS
A. Floor Map — pg. 68, #5
B. Bible Story Cards — pg. 69, #11
C. Narration — pg. 70, #14

3. MEMORY OBJECT: Sandals
Giveaway: A sandal key chain
Story/Object Association: The parting of the Jordan River when the priests stepped into the water

4. REVIEW QUESTIONS
1. Who was the Israelites' leader after Moses died? (**Joshua**)
2. Where were the Israelites finally going to enter? (**Canaan/The Promised Land**)
3. What river did the Israelites need to cross? (**The Jordan River**)
4. Who went into the river first? (**The priests**)
5. What happened when they touched the water? (**The river separated**)

Life Application Question: How do we know that God keeps His promises? (**We can read in the Bible to see how He kept them in the past and know that He will do the same in the future.**)

5. PRAYER FOCUS
Faith to know that God will keep His promises

REVIEW & MEMORY TIME

REVIEW OPTIONS:
- Name Scramble
  pg. 108, #7
- Bible Pictionary
  pg. 108, #9
- Shaving Cream Review
  pg. 110, #18
- Story Review Cards
  pg. 111, #23

MEMORY VERSE OPTIONS:
- Clue Word Memory Cards
  pg. 114, #8
- Memory Verse Square
  pg. 116, #17
- Name That Verse
  pg. 118, #23

MEMORY OBJECT OPTIONS:
- Object Match
  pg. 119, #2
- Object Poster
  pg. 120, #7

FALL OF JERICHO

27

STORY REFERENCE: Joshua 6
MEMORY VERSE: Hebrews 11:30 — By faith the walls of Jericho fell, after the people had marched around them for seven days.

STORYTELLING TIME

1. TO THE STORYTELLER
BEFORE YOU BEGIN: Ask review questions from the previous ten stories.
Having faith in God isn't always easy because we have to believe in something we cannot see. Many people have a hard time believing stories that have amazing circumstances; they have to see it to believe it. When God told Joshua and the Israelites to march around the city of Jericho for seven days and the walls would fall to the ground, how many of the Israelites may have said, "I'll believe it when I see it!" Through this story you can show children how God's victories over amazing circumstances in the past gives us the ability to have faith and trust in Him today and forever.

2. STORYTELLING METHODS
A. Story Tape — pg. 67, #1
B. Children As Bible Characters — pg. 67, #2
C. TV Story — pg. 70, #15

3. MEMORY OBJECT: A trumpet
Giveaway: A party horn or kazoo
Story/Object Association: When the priests blew their trumpets, and the walls of Jericho fell

4. REVIEW QUESTIONS
1. What land did God promise to the Israelites? (**Canaan**)
2. Who already lived in the land? (**The Canaanites**)
3. What was the first city the Israelites conquered? (**Jericho**)
4. What did the Israelites do for six days? (**They marched around the city, one time each day.**)
5. What happened to the city on the seventh day? (**The walls fell down.**)

Life Application Question: What does it mean to have faith? (**To believe that God is always with you and will do what is best for you.**)

5. PRAYER FOCUS
Faith and trust in God

REVIEW & MEMORY TIME

REVIEW OPTIONS:
- Card Scramble
  pg. 107, #1
- Beach Ball Review
  pg. 109, #15
- Card Collection
  pg. 110, #20
- Change the Bible Story
  pg. 112, #28

MEMORY VERSE OPTIONS:
- Memory Verse Mix
  pg. 113, #2
- Guess a Letter
  pg. 115, #13
- Memory Choir
  pg. 115, #15

MEMORY OBJECT OPTIONS:
- Object Bag
  pg. 119, #3
- Memory Object Bookmark
  pg. 120, #9

28 ACHAN

STORY REFERENCE: Joshua 7
MEMORY VERSE: Romans 6:23 — For the wages of sin is death, but the gift of God is eternal life in Christ Jesus our Lord.

STORYTELLING TIME

1. TO THE STORYTELLER
BEFORE YOU BEGIN: Ask review questions from the previous ten stories.
Most of the time you can tell when children are trying to hide something. They act a little nervous and are very secretive. Many times children try to hide things from the people they love and respect because they don't want to disappoint them. As adults, we may sometimes try to do the same with God. This biblical story is a perfect example for showing children that you can't hide anything from God because He knows everything that you do. It is always better to be honest and confess your sins.

2. STORYTELLING METHODS
A. Storyteller As a Bible Character — pg. 67, #3
B. Storytelling Puppet — pg. 68, #8
C. Bible Time Machine — pg. 69, #12

3. MEMORY OBJECT: A candy coin wrapped in gold foil or play money
Giveaway: A candy coin wrapped in gold foil
Story/Object Association: The gold that Achan took from Jericho

4. REVIEW QUESTIONS
1. What city did the Israelites conquer? **(Jericho)**
2. Why didn't the Israelites win the battle at Ai? **(Because one Israelite disobeyed God and took some valuables from Jericho)**
3. Who took some valuables to keep for himself? **(Achan)**
4. What things did he take? **(Gold, silver, and a robe)**
5. How was he punished for his sin? **(He and his family were stoned to death.)**

Life Application Question: Why do people try to hide sin from God? **(Because they are ashamed of their sin)**

5. PRAYER FOCUS
Confession of sins

REVIEW & MEMORY TIME

REVIEW OPTIONS:
- Character Quotes
  pg. 108, #8
- What Am I?
  pg. 108, #10
- Guess My Name
  pg. 109, #11
- Bible Story Bag
  pg. 112, #27

MEMORY VERSE OPTIONS:
- Memory Verse Card Drill
  pg. 113, #4
- Catch a Verse
  pg. 115, #12
- Memory Verse Puppet
  pg. 117, #19

MEMORY OBJECT OPTIONS:
- Name That Object
  pg. 119, #4
- Object Sequence
  pg. 119, #5

GIDEON

29

STORY REFERENCE: Judges 6 – 7
MEMORY VERSE: 1 Corinthians 1:27 — But God chose the foolish things of the world to shame the wise; God chose the weak things of the world to shame the strong.

STORYTELLING TIME

1. TO THE STORYTELLER
BEFORE YOU BEGIN: Ask review questions from the previous ten stories.
How many times do we find ourselves thinking or saying, "Please don't ask me do that; I don't think I can!" Moses and Gideon are two people who felt this way when God asked them to do very difficult tasks. God used these men to further His kingdom, even though they didn't feel capable of doing the job. Use this story to show your children that God is creative and uses very unlikely people to do great things. God may choose the most unlikely child you can think of to be the Billy Graham of the twenty-first century!

2. STORYTELLING METHODS
A. Seat Performers — pg. 68, #6
B. Bible Story Apron — pg. 69, #10
C. Narration — pg. 70, #14

3. MEMORY OBJECT: A large candle
GIVEAWAY: A small candle
STORY/OBJECT ASSOCIATION: The lanterns that Gideon and his men took with them when they invaded the Midianite camp

4. REVIEW QUESTIONS
1. What did God choose Gideon to do? (**Lead an attack on the Midianites**)
2. How many men attacked the Midianite camp? (**Three hundred**)
3. What three things did each man take with him? (**A trumpet, jar, and torch**)
4. How did Gideon defeat the Midianites? (**God helped Gideon's army to scare the Midianites**)
5. The story of Gideon is found in what book? (**Judges**)

LIFE APPLICATION QUESTION: Whom can God use to further His kingdom?
(**Anyone who will obey Him**)

5. PRAYER FOCUS
How God can use each child in some type of ministry

REVIEW & MEMORY TIME

REVIEW OPTIONS:
- Bible Basketball
  pg. 107, #6
- Guess My Name
  pg. 109, #11
- Bible Charades
  pg. 109, #14
- Card Collection
  pg. 110, #20

MEMORY VERSE OPTIONS:
- Memory Verse Pocket
  pg. 113, #6
- Memory Balloon-a-Thon
  pg. 115, #11
- Memory Verse Sticks
  pg. 117, #20

MEMORY OBJECT OPTIONS:
- Bible Biography
  pg. 119, #1
- Musical Objects
  pg. 119, #6

GIDEON
OLD TESTAMENT

30 SAMSON

STORY REFERENCE: Judges 16
MEMORY VERSE: Ephesians 6:10 — Finally, be strong in the Lord and in his mighty power.

STORYTELLING TIME

1. TO THE STORYTELLER
BEFORE YOU BEGIN: Ask review questions from the previous ten stories.
The life application question for this story is "How can a person lose his Christian strength?" The importance of this story is for children to understand that when their focus is not on God and when they don't put Him first in their lives, their Christian strength and witness are in jeopardy. When they realize that their strength is gone, all they have to do is ask, like Samson, and God will lead them on the right path to build them up once again.

2. STORYTELLING METHODS
A. Story Tape — pg. 67, #1
B. Bible Story Cards — pg. 69, #11
C. TV Story — pg. 70, #15

3. MEMORY OBJECT: A pair of scissors
GIVEAWAY: A pair of children's scissors
STORY/OBJECT ASSOCIATION: When the Philistines cut Samson's hair

4. REVIEW QUESTIONS
1. Who was the woman Samson loved? **(Delilah)**
2. Why did she want Samson to tell her his secret? **(Because the Philistines promised to give her money if she could find out Samson's secret)**
3. What was the secret of Samson's strength? **(The fact that his hair had never been cut)**
4. What did the Philistines do to Samson? **(They gouged out his eyes.)**
5. How did Samson kill the people at the temple? **(He pushed the temple pillars apart and the temple fell to the ground.)**

Life Application Question: How can we lose our Christian strength? **(By not growing in our relationship with God through prayer, reading the Bible, and serving God)**

5. PRAYER FOCUS
Christian strength for each child

REVIEW & MEMORY TIME

REVIEW OPTIONS:
- Bible Pictionary pg. 108, #9
- Bible Time Capsule pg. 110, #21
- Story Diorama pg. 111, #22
- Story Card Match pg. 111, #25

MEMORY VERSE OPTIONS:
- Memory Verse Envelope pg. 113, #3
- Chalkboard Verse pg. 114, #10
- Memory Verse Bulletin Board pg. 118, #24

MEMORY OBJECT OPTIONS:
- Name That Object pg. 119, #4
- Object Mural pg. 120, #8

RUTH & NAOMI

31

STORY REFERENCE: Ruth 1
MEMORY VERSE: Ruth 1:16 — But Ruth replied, "Don't urge me to leave you or to turn back from you. Where you go I will go, and where you stay I will stay. Your people will be my people and your God my God."

STORYTELLING TIME

1. TO THE STORYTELLER
BEFORE YOU BEGIN: Ask review questions from the previous ten stories.
God allowing His only Son to be sacrificed on the cross for our sins is the ultimate story of love. The story of Ruth and Naomi shows us a kind of love that one human being can have for another. Children, especially those from broken homes, may have a hard time understanding unconditional love. Use this Bible story to show children that God loves each of us, even more than Ruth loved Naomi. He loves and accepts us just the way we are, and His love is forever.

2. STORYTELLING METHODS
A. Children As Bible Characters — pg. 67, #2
B. Floor Map — pg. 68, #5
C. Narration — pg. 70, #14

3. MEMORY OBJECT: A map or airline baggage tag
Giveaway: A map
Story/Object Association: Ruth and Naomi's travel back to Bethlehem

4. REVIEW QUESTIONS
1. Who were Naomi's daughters-in-law? **(Ruth and Orpah)**
2. What happened to Naomi's husband and sons? **(They died.)**
3. Where did Naomi beg the women to go? **(Back to their families)**
4. Which daughter-in-law stayed with Naomi? **(Ruth)**
5. What famous king was Ruth's grandson? **(King David)**

Life Application Question: Who are the people that love you? *(Allow for a variety of answers.)*

5. PRAYER FOCUS
Love for others

REVIEW & MEMORY TIME

REVIEW OPTIONS:
- Card Scramble
  pg. 107, #1
- Newspaper Search
  pg. 110, #17
- Bible Story Map
  pg. 111, #24
- Bible Story Mural
  pg. 111, #26

MEMORY VERSE OPTIONS:
- Memory Verse Match
  pg. 114, #7
- Memory Ladder
  pg. 116, #16
- Memory Verse Golf
  pg. 116, #18

MEMORY OBJECT OPTIONS:
- Object Poster
  pg. 120, #7
- Memory Object Bookmark
  pg. 120, #9

32 SAMUEL'S CALL

Story Reference: 1 Samuel 3
Memory Verse: Jeremiah 29:11 — "For I know the plans I have for you," declares the LORD, "plans to prosper you and not to harm you, plans to give you hope and a future."

STORYTELLING TIME

1. TO THE STORYTELLER
BEFORE YOU BEGIN: Ask review questions from the previous ten stories. Before you tell this story, pray that God will bless you and touch the hearts of the children to whom you will be speaking. God wants to use you in a mighty way as you tell the story of "Samuel's Call." Make it a story that the children will never forget. With this story, you have a unique opportunity to plant a seed that will grow in the heart of a child who may sometime soon feel a call into full-time Christian ministry. What an awesome and exciting task!

2. STORYTELLING METHODS
A. Children As Bible Characters — pg. 67, #2
B. Seat Performers — pg. 68, #6
C. SuperCards/Overhead Transparencies — pg. 70, #13

3. MEMORY OBJECT: A telephone or pillow
Giveaway: A Whatchama*call*it candy bar
Story/Object Association: God calling Samuel

4. REVIEW QUESTIONS
1. What did Hannah ask God to give her? (**A son**)
2. What did Hannah name her son? (**Samuel**)
3. Where was Samuel taken when he was young? (**To the temple**)
4. Who was really calling to Samuel? (**God**)
5. What jobs did Samuel have when he grew up? (**Prophet, priest, and judge**)

Life Application Question: Has God called you yet? (*You can ask the children specific questions, like, "Do you think God wants you to be a preacher or missionary, or to serve in another full-time ministry?"*)

5. PRAYER FOCUS
That each child will listen for and obey God's call upon his or her life

REVIEW & MEMORY TIME

REVIEW OPTIONS:
- Card Scramble
  pg. 107, #1
- Bible Pictionary
  pg. 108, #9
- Who Am I?
  pg. 110, #16
- Story Card Spinner
  pg. 110, #19

MEMORY VERSE OPTIONS:
- Clothespin Review
  pg. 113, #5
- Catch a Verse
  pg. 115, #12
- Memory Choir
  pg. 115, #15

MEMORY OBJECT OPTIONS:
- Object Match
  pg. 119, #2
- Object Sequence
  pg. 119, #5

SAMUEL ANOINTS SAUL — 33

STORY REFERENCE: 1 Samuel 8 – 10
MEMORY VERSE: John 15:19b — As it is, you do not belong to the world, but I have chosen you out of the world.

STORYTELLING TIME

1. TO THE STORYTELLER
BEFORE YOU BEGIN: Ask review questions from the previous ten stories.
Children love to be chosen to do a special job. It makes them proud and their self-esteem is elevated. This story can help them to relate to Saul when he was chosen by God to be the first king of Israel. Like Saul, God has chosen each one of the children to do a special job for His kingdom. No matter how important the job is, or how difficult it may be, God will always be with them.

2. STORYTELLING METHODS
A. Story Tape — pg. 67, #1
B. Draw a Picture — pg. 68, #7
C. SuperCards/Overhead Transparencies — pg. 70, #13

3. MEMORY OBJECT: A Head and Shoulders shampoo bottle
Giveaway: A trial-size bottle of shampoo
Story/Object Association: Saul's being a head taller than the other men

4. REVIEW QUESTIONS
1. What job did Samuel have for many years? **(Judge of Israel)**
2. What did the Israelites tell Samuel they wanted? **(A king)**
3. Who was chosen to be the first king of Israel? **(Saul)**
4. What did Samuel pour over Saul's head? Why? **(Oil; to show that Saul had been anointed king)**
5. What did Samuel go back and tell the Israelites? **(That God had chosen Saul to be their first king)**

Life Application Question: What have you been chosen for? *(You may get several answers, like, "line leader/special helper at school.")*

5. PRAYER FOCUS
That each child will be what God wants him or her to be

REVIEW & MEMORY TIME

REVIEW OPTIONS:
- Card Scramble
  pg. 107, #1
- What Am I?
  pg. 108, #10
- Bible Baseball
  pg. 109, #12
- Beach Ball Review
  pg. 109, #15

MEMORY VERSE OPTIONS:
- Memory Verse Mix
  pg. 113, #2
- Pass the Hat
  pg. 114, #9
- Memory Verse Mobile
  pg. 117, #22

MEMORY OBJECT OPTIONS:
- Object Bag
  pg. 119, #3
- Object Poster
  pg. 120, #7

34 SAMUEL ANOINTS DAVID

STORY REFERENCE: 1 Samuel 15 – 16
MEMORY VERSE: 1 Samuel 15:22a — Does the LORD delight in burnt offerings and sacrifices as much as in obeying the voice of the LORD?

STORYTELLING TIME

1. TO THE STORYTELLER
BEFORE YOU BEGIN: Ask review questions from the previous ten stories. Children who grow up in homes where disobedience is seldom corrected do not understand what it means to suffer consequences for their inappropriate behavior. This Bible story is powerful in showing that when people choose to disobey God, there will always be consequences. Saul's punishment was severe — he ended up losing his throne.

2. STORYTELLING METHODS
A. Children As Bible Characters — pg. 67, #2
B. Draw a Picture — pg. 68, #7
C. Narration — pg. 70, #14

3. MEMORY OBJECT: A bottle of baby oil or a can of motor oil
Giveaway: A trial-size bottle of baby oil or lotion
Story/Object Association: Samuel's anointing David with oil

4. REVIEW QUESTIONS
1. Why could Saul no longer be the king of Israel? **(He disobeyed God)**
2. Why was Samuel supposed to go to Bethlehem? **(To meet Jesse)**
3. How many sons did Jesse have? **(Eight)**
4. Who did God choose to be the new king? **(David)**
5. What did Samuel do to the new king? **(Samuel anointed him with oil.)**

Life Application Question: What happens when we disobey, like Saul did? **(God disciplines us for sinning.)**

5. PRAYER FOCUS
Wisdom to know what is right and not to disobey

REVIEW & MEMORY TIME

REVIEW OPTIONS:
- Bible Bingo
  pg. 107, #5
- Character Quotes
  pg. 108, #8
- Balloon Pop Review
  pg. 109, #13
- Story Review Cards
  pg. 111, #23

MEMORY VERSE OPTIONS:
- Memory Verse Match
  pg. 114, #7
- Chalkboard Verse
  pg. 114, #10
- Memory Verse Square
  pg. 116, #17

MEMORY OBJECT OPTIONS:
- Bible Biography
  pg. 119, #1
- Musical Objects
  pg. 119, #6

DAVID & GOLIATH

35

STORY REFERENCE: 1 Samuel 17
MEMORY VERSE: John 17:15 — My prayer is not that you take them out of the world but that you protect them from the evil one.

STORYTELLING TIME

1. TO THE STORYTELLER
BEFORE YOU BEGIN: Ask review questions from the previous ten stories.
This popular story teaches several principles: serving others, taking a stand for God, being ready to do what God calls us to do, and seeing how God uses our past experiences to prepare us for the future. This story is great for helping kids to see how Satan wants to keep us from applying these principles to our lives. Sometimes Satan tries to defeat us through difficult situations or through the words of other people which may hurt us. But, like David, if we call upon the name of the Lord we can overcome our enemy (Satan) just as David overcame Goliath.

2. STORYTELLING METHODS
A. Storyteller As a Bible Character — pg. 67, #3
B. Bible Story Apron — pg. 69, #10
C. Bible Time Machine — pg. 69, #12

3. MEMORY OBJECT: A slingshot
GIVEAWAY: A small, round stone or a slingshot
STORY/OBJECT ASSOCIATION: What David used to kill Goliath

4. REVIEW QUESTIONS
1. What was the name of the giant Philistine? (**Goliath**)
2. What did he do to make David angry? (**He said bad things about God's army.**)
3. How tall was the giant? (**Over nine feet tall**)
4. Who killed the giant? (**David**)
5. How did the giant die? (**David threw a stone that hit Goliath in the forehead.**)

LIFE APPLICATION QUESTION: Who is the giant enemy we face? (**Satan**)

5. PRAYER FOCUS
Courage and wisdom in facing our giants

REVIEW & MEMORY TIME

REVIEW OPTIONS:
- Card Scramble
  pg. 107, #1
- Who Am I?
  pg. 110, #16
- Story Card Spinner
  pg. 110, #19
- Story Diorama
  pg. 111, #22

MEMORY VERSE OPTIONS:
- Memory Verse Card Drill
  pg. 113, #4
- Memory Verse Golf
  pg. 116, #18
- Memory Verse Puppet
  pg. 117, #19

MEMORY OBJECT OPTIONS:
- Object Sequence
  pg. 119, #5
- Memory Object Bookmark
  pg. 120, #9

36 DAVID SPARES SAUL

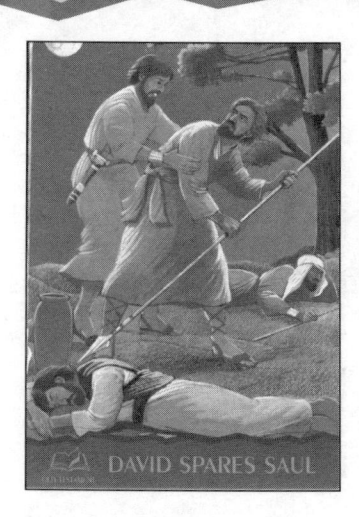

STORY REFERENCE: 1 Samuel 26
MEMORY VERSE: Romans 12:17 — Do not repay anyone evil for evil. Be careful to do what is right in the eyes of everybody.

STORYTELLING TIME

1. **TO THE STORYTELLER**

    BEFORE YOU BEGIN: Ask review questions from the previous ten stories. Bullies abound. We've all had one in our lives. Saul was a bully toward David. He set out to kill David, but David refused to retaliate and kill Saul. David showed kindness toward his "bully." He saw Saul as someone chosen by God for a particular and unique purpose. And even though Saul turned evil, David knew he should not harm God's chosen. David tried to reconcile with Saul, and, when that didn't work, David avoided Saul and encouraged others not to treat Saul with contempt. In today's atmosphere of violence and vengeance, we need to take a strong stand against the attitude or action of retaliation.

2. **STORYTELLING METHODS**
    A. Storytelling Puppet — pg. 68, #8
    B. Spray Can Storytelling — pg. 69, #9
    C. Bible Story Cards — pg. 69, #11

3. **MEMORY OBJECT:** A spear
    Giveaway: A piece of *spear*mint gum
    Story/Object Association: The spear that Abishai and David took from King Saul

4. **REVIEW QUESTIONS**
    1. Why was Saul jealous of David? **(Because David was very successful)**
    2. Why did David have to hide from Saul? **(Because Saul was trying to kill him)**
    3. Who pulled out a spear to kill Saul? **(Abishai)**
    4. What did David take from Saul? **(Saul's spear and water jug)**
    5. What did Saul realize the next day? **(That David could have killed him but instead spared his life)**

    Life Application Question: How should we treat people who are mean? **(We should love them as we love ourselves.)**

5. **PRAYER FOCUS**
    Overcoming the attitude or action of being unkind to others

REVIEW & MEMORY TIME

REVIEW OPTIONS:
- Card Scramble pg. 107, #1
- Give Me a Clue pg. 107, #2
- Bible Story Bag pg. 112, #27
- Change the Bible Story pg. 112, #28

MEMORY VERSE OPTIONS:
- Memory Balloon-a-Thon pg. 115, #11
- Round Table Memory pg. 115, #14
- Name That Verse pg. 118, #23

MEMORY OBJECT OPTIONS:
- Object Match pg. 119, #2
- Object Bag pg. 119, #3

RETURN OF THE ARK　　37

STORY REFERENCE: 2 Samuel 6
MEMORY VERSE: John 14:23a — Jesus replied, "If anyone loves me, he will obey my teaching."

STORYTELLING TIME

1. TO THE STORYTELLER
BEFORE YOU BEGIN: Ask review questions from the previous ten stories. Authority is a part of life. We either follow those in authority over us or we don't. If we choose not to, we will experience unnecessary grief. Learning to follow earthly authority is the beginning of learning to follow God's authority. Children often misunderstand the importance of following rules and laws. They sometimes fail to see how life would be chaotic without rules. As children learn to follow earthly authority it is easier for them to follow God's commands. Today you have the opportunity to help children see that God's commands guide and protect us.

2. STORYTELLING METHODS
A. Floor Map — pg. 68, #5
B. Seat Performers — pg. 68, #6
C. Bible Story Cards — pg. 69, #11

3. MEMORY OBJECT: A jewelry box or a treasure chest
GIVEAWAY: A small treasure chest
STORY/OBJECT ASSOCIATION: The ark of the covenant

4. REVIEW QUESTIONS
1. Who was the king of Israel before David? **(Saul)**
2. Who had taken the ark from the Israelites? **(The Philistines)**
3. How did David move the ark the first time? **(With a cart)**
4. What was the correct way to move the ark? **(It was to be carried by the poles and never to be touched.)**
5. How did David show that he was happy? **(He danced for joy.)**

LIFE APPLICATION QUESTION: What should we do with God's commands? **(We should obey them.)**

5. PRAYER FOCUS
Obedience to the truth of what we know we should or shouldn't do

REVIEW & MEMORY TIME

REVIEW OPTIONS:
- Name Scramble
  pg. 108, #7
- Character Quotes
  pg. 108, #8
- Newspaper Search
  pg. 110, #17
- Story Review Cards
  pg. 111, #23

MEMORY VERSE OPTIONS:
- Memory Verse Envelope
  pg. 113, #3
- Guess a Letter
  pg. 115, #13
- Memory Verse Bulletin Board
  pg. 118, #24

MEMORY OBJECT OPTIONS:
- Name That Object
  pg. 119, #4
- Object Poster
  pg. 120, #7

38 BUILDING THE TEMPLE

Story Reference: 1 Kings 6
Memory Verse: John 4:24 — God is spirit, and his worshipers must worship in spirit and in truth.

STORYTELLING TIME

1. TO THE STORYTELLER
BEFORE YOU BEGIN: Ask review questions from the previous ten stories.
When we go to the store, we buy things we need. When we go to school, we learn. When we go to church, we worship God. The practice of worshiping God means to apply worth to God. When we go to church to worship, we are giving God our "worth-ship." The building we worship in has changed since the days of the Temple, but the importance of worship has not. God wants us to come together to worship Him. By worshiping God with others, we are strengthened in our faith, encouraged to continue serving Him, and challenged to change the areas of our lives with which God is displeased.

2. STORYTELLING METHODS
A. Map It Out — pg. 67, #4
B. SuperCards/Overhead Transparencies — pg. 70, #13
C. Narration — pg. 70, #14

3. MEMORY OBJECT: A sponge "brick"
Giveaway: A red sponge
Story/Object Association: The bricks that were used to build the Temple

4. REVIEW QUESTIONS
1. Which of David's sons became the new king? (**Solomon**)
2. What did God say the new king would build? (**A temple**)
3. Whom was the Temple specifically built for? (**God**)
4. What didn't the workers do at the building site? (**They did not make any hammering or chiseling noises.**)
5. How was the inside of the Temple decorated? (**Everything was covered in solid gold.**)

Life Application Question: Where do we worship God? (**At church** — *allow for a variety of answers*)

5. PRAYER FOCUS
Asking God to help us worship Him

REVIEW & MEMORY TIME

REVIEW OPTIONS:
- Bible Basketball
  pg. 107, #6
- Shaving Cream Review
  pg. 110, #18
- Story Card Spinner
  pg. 110, #19
- Temple Model
  pg. 112, #30

MEMORY VERSE OPTIONS:
- Memory Verse Pocket
  pg. 113, #6
- Memory Ladder
  pg. 116, #16
- Memory Verse Sticks
  pg. 117, #20

MEMORY OBJECT OPTIONS:
- Bible Biography
  pg. 119, #1
- Musical Objects
  pg. 119, #6

RAVENS FEED ELIJAH

39

Story Reference: 1 Kings 17:1-6
Memory Verse: Philippians 4:19 — And my God will meet all your needs according to his glorious riches in Christ Jesus.

STORYTELLING TIME

1. TO THE STORYTELLER
BEFORE YOU BEGIN: Ask review questions from the previous ten stories.
Jehovah Jireh is a Hebrew phrase which means "God is my provider." Sometimes it is difficult to see how God is going to meet needs, but in this story we see how God was Elijah's provider in a unique way. Through Elijah's obedience and God's faithfulness, the necessary provision was made for Elijah. God knows what we need before we ask and will meet our needs according to His will for our lives. Children need help in understanding the difference between wants and needs. Wants are the things we would like to have but don't need. Needs are things we must have to survive (food, clothing, shelter) and things which God wants us to have in order to do His work.

2. STORYTELLING METHODS
A. Story Tape — pg. 67, #1
B. Seat Performers — pg. 68, #6
C. Bible Story Apron — pg. 69, #10

3. MEMORY OBJECT: Oyster crackers
Giveaway: A few oyster crackers
Story/Object Association: The bread which the ravens brought for Elijah to eat

4. REVIEW QUESTIONS
1. What king did God tell Elijah to go and see? (**King Ahab**)
2. What is a prophet? (**A person who speaks for God**)
3. What message did Elijah give to the king? (**That there would be no rain in the king's land unless Elijah told it to rain**)
4. Where did Elijah hide? (**In a ravine**)
5. How did God provide food for Elijah to eat? (**God had some ravens take food to Elijah.**)

Life Application Question: What does God provide for you? (**Food, clothes, shelter** — *allow for a variety of answers*)

5. PRAYER FOCUS
Thankfulness to God for providing what we need

REVIEW & MEMORY TIME

REVIEW OPTIONS:
- Bible Tic-Tac-Toe
  pg. 107, #4
- Bible Baseball
  pg. 109, #12
- Beach Ball Review
  pg. 109, #15
- Bible Story Bag
  pg. 112, #27

MEMORY VERSE OPTIONS:
- Clothespin Review
  pg. 113, #5
- Clue Word Memory Cards
  pg. 114, #8
- Balloon Pop Race
  pg. 117, #21

MEMORY OBJECT OPTIONS:
- Object Sequence
  pg. 119, #5
- Memory Object Bookmark
  pg. 120, #9

40 FIRE FROM HEAVEN

Story Reference: 1 Kings 18:16-45
Memory Verse: Matthew 7:7 — Ask and it will be given to you; seek and you will find; knock and the door will be opened to you.

STORYTELLING TIME

1. TO THE STORYTELLER
BEFORE YOU BEGIN: Ask review questions from the previous ten stories.
Prayer is the vital connection between God and His people. This story is a classic encounter where prayer of faith prevails. To insure a right relationship with God, it is important to pray (talk) to Him on a regular basis. Just as God honored Elijah's prayer, He will honor our prayers. This story can be used to heighten children's interest in prayer and to demonstrate prayer's fantastic results.

2. STORYTELLING METHODS
A. Storytelling Puppet — pg. 68, #8
B. Bible Story Cards — pg. 69, #11
C. TV Story — pg. 70, #15

3. MEMORY OBJECT: Caramel candies
Giveaway: A piece of caramel candy
Story/Object Association: Mount Carmel, where Elijah prayed for God to light the wood on his altar

4. REVIEW QUESTIONS
1. Who did King Ahab worship? **(Baal)**
2. What did Elijah want to prove to King Ahab? **(That Baal was not real)**
3. How did Baal's prophets pray to their god? **(They shouted, danced, and sang.)**
4. What happened when Baal's prophets prayed? **(Nothing)**
5. What happened when Elijah prayed to God? **(God lit the wood on the altar, and the fire consumed the sacrifice and the water in the ditch around the altar.)**

Life Application Question: What prayer has God answered for you? *(Allow for a variety of answers.)*

5. PRAYER FOCUS
Praise to God for hearing and answering prayers

REVIEW & MEMORY TIME

REVIEW OPTIONS:
- Guess My Name
  pg. 109, #11
- Bible Charades
  pg. 109, #14
- Bible Time Capsule
  pg. 110, #21
- Story Card Match
  pg. 111, #25

MEMORY VERSE OPTIONS:
- Memory Verse Book
  pg. 113, #1
- Catch a Verse
  pg. 115, #12
- Memory Verse Square
  pg. 116, #17

MEMORY OBJECT OPTIONS:
- Name That Object
  pg. 119, #4
- Object Mural
  pg. 120, #8

NAAMAN

41

STORY REFERENCE: 2 Kings 5
MEMORY VERSE: James 4:10 — Humble yourselves before the Lord, and he will lift you up.

STORYTELLING TIME

1. TO THE STORYTELLER
BEFORE YOU BEGIN: Ask review questions from the previous ten stories.
Some kids (most kids) like to get dirty. It is a lot of fun for kids to get grimy and slimy. But not Naaman — he was a man of high ranking, the commander of the Syrian army. For him to go into the dirty water was a very humbling experience. He probably felt like he was too important to go into the river. This is a good lesson on "swallowing pride" and doing what is right. Children face moments of pride which may interfere with their relationship with God or hinder them in making right decisions.

2. STORYTELLING METHODS
A. Storyteller As a Bible Character — pg. 67, #3
B. Bible Time Machine — pg. 69, #12
C. TV Story — pg. 70, #15

3. MEMORY OBJECT: A bar of soap
GIVEAWAY: A hotel-sized bar of soap
Story/Object Association: Naaman washing in the river

4. REVIEW QUESTIONS
1. What disease did Naaman have? (**Leprosy**)
2. Whom did the servant girl want Naaman to see? (**Elisha, the prophet**)
3. What did the prophet tell Naaman? (**That if Naaman would wash in the Jordan River seven times, he would be cured**)
4. What did Naaman think of this? (**He didn't want to wash in the river because it was muddy and dirty.**)
5. When was Naaman healed from his disease? (**After he washed seven times**)

LIFE APPLICATION QUESTION: What does it mean to be proud? (**Being proud is thinking that you are better than others.**)

5. PRAYER FOCUS
Repentance of pride

REVIEW & MEMORY TIME

REVIEW OPTIONS:
- Name Scramble
  pg. 108, #7
- Bible Pictionary
  pg. 108, #9
- Balloon Pop Review
  pg. 109, #13
- Bible Story Mural
  pg. 111, #26

MEMORY VERSE OPTIONS:
- Pass the Hat
  pg. 114, #9
- Memory Ladder
  pg. 116, #16
- Memory Verse Puppet
  pg. 117, #19

MEMORY OBJECT OPTIONS:
- Object Bag
  pg. 119, #3
- Musical Objects
  pg. 119, #6

42 JOASH

STORY REFERENCE: 2 Kings 11
MEMORY VERSE: Isaiah 11:6b — And a little child will lead them.

STORYTELLING TIME

1. TO THE STORYTELLER
BEFORE YOU BEGIN: Ask review questions from the previous ten stories. Children often dream of being "in charge" and what they would do if they could make the rules. Joash was seven years old when he became king and ruled over Israel. Even though he was king, Jehoiada the priest helped Joash to rule the people. As a seven-year-old, he needed a lot of guidance in his early years as king. This is true of children today. They need to be encouraged to follow the guidance of parents, pastors, and teachers — even if they are anointed "king."

2. STORYTELLING METHODS
A. Children As Bible Characters — pg. 67, #2
B. Storytelling Puppet — pg. 68, #8
C. TV Story — pg. 70, #15

3. MEMORY OBJECT: A Burger King crown
Giveaway: A Burger King crown
Story/Object Association: Joash's being crowned king

4. REVIEW QUESTIONS
1. Why did the evil queen want to kill Joash? (**So that Joash wouldn't become the new king**)
2. Who saved Joash from the queen? (**His aunt**)
3. Where was Joash hidden? (**In the Temple**)
4. What happened to the evil queen? (**She was killed.**)
5. How old was Joash when he was crowned king? (**Seven years old**)

Life Application Question: What would you do if you were a king? (*Allow for a variety of reasonable answers.*)

5. PRAYER FOCUS
Thanking God for leaders, and asking for God's protection and wisdom for them as they lead

REVIEW & MEMORY TIME

REVIEW OPTIONS:
- Give Me a Clue
  pg. 107, #2
- Bible Baseball
  pg. 109, #12
- Bible Charades
  pg. 109, #14
- Change the Bible Story
  pg. 112, #28

MEMORY VERSE OPTIONS:
- Memory Verse Envelope
  pg. 113, #3
- Guess a Letter
  pg. 115, #13
- Round Table Memory
  pg. 115, #14

MEMORY OBJECT OPTIONS:
- Bible Biography
  pg. 119, #1
- Object Match
  pg. 119, #2

JOB

43

STORY REFERENCE: Job 1 – 42
MEMORY VERSE: 1 Corinthians 10:13b — And God is faithful; he will not let you be tempted beyond what you can bear.

STORYTELLING TIME

1. TO THE STORYTELLER
BEFORE YOU BEGIN: Ask review questions from the previous ten stories.
Everyone is tempted. Children even come to the point of trying to decide what to do when confronted with decisions between right and wrong. But different people handle temptation differently. For instance, one person may be tempted and successfully resist that temptation. However, another person may be tempted and give in to that temptation. In this story, temptation runs alongside adversity. Job reminds us to confront temptation and always to do what is right, even when life seems unfair and unkind.

2. STORYTELLING METHODS
A. Story Tape — pg. 67, #1
B. Storyteller As a Bible Character — pg. 67, #3
C. SuperCards/Overhead Transparencies — pg. 70, #13

3. MEMORY OBJECT: A box of bandage strips
Giveaway: A bandage strip
Story/Object Association: The sores that Job had all over his body

4. REVIEW QUESTIONS
1. What did Satan get permission to do to Job? **(Tempt him)**
2. What was Satan not allowed to do? **(Kill Job)**
3. What things did Satan take away from Job? **(Family, servants, animals)**
4. What did Job's wife want him to do? **(Curse God and die)**
5. How did God bless Job? **(God gave Job back twice as much as he had lost.)**

Life Application Question: How does Satan tempt us? **(By trying to get us to say mean things to others, not to spend time with God, to do things that go against God —** *allow for a variety of answers.***)**

5. PRAYER FOCUS
Strength to overcome our temptations

REVIEW & MEMORY TIME

REVIEW OPTIONS:
- Overhead Game
    pg. 107, #3
- Character Quotes
    pg. 108, #8
- Bible Time Capsule
    pg. 110, #21
- Bible Story Bag
    pg. 112, #27

MEMORY VERSE OPTIONS:
- Memory Verse Match
    pg. 114, #7
- Chalkboard Verse
    pg. 114, #10
- Memory Verse Bulletin Board
    pg. 118, #24

MEMORY OBJECT OPTIONS:
- Object Sequence
    pg. 119, #5
- Object Poster
    pg. 120, #7

44 JONAH

STORY REFERENCE: Jonah 1 – 4
MEMORY VERSE: Jonah 1:3a — But Jonah ran away from the LORD and headed for Tarshish.

STORYTELLING TIME

1. TO THE STORYTELLER
BEFORE YOU BEGIN: Ask review questions from the previous ten stories.
A train is very powerful as long as it stays on railroad tracks. Once off the tracks, the train loses its power because it can no longer move. This means the train cannot fulfill its purpose. Jonah was like a train off the tracks. Because he was running from God he was operating on his own limited power, rather than the power of God. Jonah's story helps children to see why each of us needs to stay on track with God.

2. STORYTELLING METHODS
A. Floor Map — pg. 68, #5
B. Seat Performers — pg. 68, #6
C. Narration — pg. 70, #14

3. MEMORY OBJECT: A box of fish crackers
GIVEAWAY: A few fish crackers
Story/Object Association: Jonah's being swallowed by a fish

4. REVIEW QUESTIONS
1. Where did God ask Jonah to go and preach? **(Nineveh)**
2. Why did Jonah try to run away from God? **(Jonah didn't want to preach to the people at Nineveh.)**
3. What did the crew members do to calm the sea? **(They threw Jonah overboard.)**
4. What happened while Jonah was in the water? **(He was swallowed by a fish.)**
5. What happened when Jonah went to Nineveh? **(All of the people in the city asked God to forgive them of their sins.)**

Life Application Question: Why do people sometimes run away from God? **(Because they are afraid or do not want to do what God asks of them.)**

5. PRAYER FOCUS
Hearing and obeying God's call to serve Him

REVIEW & MEMORY TIME

REVIEW OPTIONS:
- Guess My Name
  pg. 109, #11
- Story Diorama
  pg. 111, #22
- Story Review Cards
  pg. 111, #23
- Bible Story Map
  pg. 111, #24

MEMORY VERSE OPTIONS:
- Memory Verse Card Drill
  pg. 113, #4
- Memory Balloon-a-Thon
  pg. 115, #11
- Memory Verse Golf
  pg. 116, #18

MEMORY OBJECT OPTIONS:
- Object Match
  pg. 119, #2
- Memory Object Bookmark
  pg. 120, #9

ISAIAH'S VISION

45

STORY REFERENCE: Isaiah 6:1-8

MEMORY VERSE: Isaiah 6:8 — Then I heard the voice of the Lord saying, "Whom shall I send? And who will go for us?" And I said, "Here am I. Send me!"

STORYTELLING TIME

1. TO THE STORYTELLER
BEFORE YOU BEGIN: Ask review questions from the previous ten stories.
This is a great story for encouraging children to be called out to serve God, either in a full-time vocation, such as pastoring, Christian education, missions, or in other areas of Christian service. Children need to be called out for service to the Lord for the future as well as the present. That is, they need to do those things which can be done right now to grow spiritually, to help others, and to make a difference right where God has placed them.

2. STORYTELLING METHODS
A. Story Tape — pg. 67, #1
B. Draw a Picture — pg. 68, #7
C. Bible Story Cards — pg. 69, #11

3. MEMORY OBJECT: A piece of charcoal
GIVEAWAY: A pair of waxed lips
Story/Object Association: When the seraph touched Isaiah's lips with the hot coal

4. REVIEW QUESTIONS
1. What is a vision? **(It is like a dream.)**
2. How did Isaiah describe God's robe? **(Isaiah said the robe was so big that it filled the Temple.)**
3. What is another name for a seraph? **(An angel)**
4. Why did the seraph touch Isaiah's lips? **(The seraph touch Isaiah's lips with the hot piece of coal to show that God wanted to take away Isaiah's sins.)**
5. What did God want Isaiah to go out and do? **(Tell others about God)**

Life Application Question: What does God call us to do today? **(He calls us to go out and tell the world about Jesus.)**

5. PRAYER FOCUS
Committing to do one thing for God this week

REVIEW & MEMORY TIME

REVIEW OPTIONS:
- Give Me a Clue
  pg. 107, #2
- Bible Basketball
  pg. 107, #6
- Newspaper Search
  pg. 110, #17
- Story Card Match
  pg. 111, #25

MEMORY VERSE OPTIONS:
- Memory Verse Pocket
  pg. 113, #6
- Memory Verse Sticks
  pg. 117, #20
- Memory Verse Mobile
  pg. 117, #22

MEMORY OBJECT OPTIONS:
- Musical Objects
  pg. 119, #6
- Object Poster
  pg. 120, #7

46 JEREMIAH

STORY REFERENCE: Jeremiah 38:1-13
MEMORY VERSE: Psalm 40:2 — He lifted me out of the slimy pit, out of the mud and mire; he set my feet on a rock and gave me a firm place to stand.

STORYTELLING TIME

1. TO THE STORYTELLER
BEFORE YOU BEGIN: Ask review questions from the previous ten stories.
At some point in their young lives, children are afraid. Kids should be able to relate to Jeremiah because he was in a scary and dangerous place. Throughout the Bible God rescues countless individuals from danger. We live in a time when it seems danger is everywhere, but God still rescues people. He promises to watch over and protect us.

2. STORYTELLING METHODS
A. Storytelling Puppet — pg. 68, #8
B. Bible Time Machine — pg. 69, #12
C. TV Story — pg. 70, #15

3. MEMORY OBJECT: A rope
Giveaway: A piece of yarn or string
Story/Object Association: The ropes used to rescue Jeremiah from the cistern

4. REVIEW QUESTIONS
1. Who was called "the weeping prophet"? (**Jeremiah**)
2. What message did he give to the Israelites? (**That they were not to fight the Babylonian army, because they would lose the fight.**)
3. Why were the king's men angry with Jeremiah? (**They said that Jeremiah didn't want anything good to happen to the Israelites.**)
4. Where did the king's men put Jeremiah? (**Into a cistern**)
5. How did they get Jeremiah out? (**They lowered ropes to him.**)

Life Application Question: Has God ever rescued you from danger? (*Allow for varied answers*)

5. PRAYER FOCUS
Thankfulness to God for rescuing us, or people we know, from danger

REVIEW & MEMORY TIME

REVIEW OPTIONS:
- Bible Tic-Tac-Toe pg. 107, #4
- Bible Baseball pg. 109, #12
- Who Am I? pg. 110, #16
- Bible Story Bag pg. 112, #27

MEMORY VERSE OPTIONS:
- Memory Verse Mix pg. 113, #2
- Memory Choir pg. 115, #15
- Name That Verse pg. 118, #23

MEMORY OBJECT OPTIONS:
- Bible Biography pg. 119, #1
- Object Bag pg. 119, #3

THE FIERY FURNACE

47

STORY REFERENCE: Daniel 3
MEMORY VERSE: Mark 12:30 — Love the Lord your God with all your heart and with all your soul and with all your mind and with all your strength.

STORYTELLING TIME

1. TO THE STORYTELLER
BEFORE YOU BEGIN: Ask review questions from the previous ten stories.
This graphic story has been a perennial favorite of children. In it, dedication and obedience to God stand out as key principles of the Christian life. As Christians we need to be reminded of the many idols screaming for our attention. Children should be encouraged not to put anything (toys, celebrities, sports, fads) above God. The "Fiery Furnace" story demonstrates how God honors those who worship Him.

2. STORYTELLING METHODS
A. Children As Bible Characters — pg. 67, #2
B. Spray Can Storytelling — pg. 69, #9
C. SuperCards/Overhead Transparencies — pg. 70, #13

3. MEMORY OBJECT: A box of matches
GIVEAWAY: A piece of cinnamon or fireball candy
STORY/OBJECT ASSOCIATION: The fiery furnace

4. REVIEW QUESTIONS
1. Who were the three Hebrew men? (**Shadrach, Meshach, and Abednego**)
2. What did the king order all of the people to do? (**Bow to his statue**)
3. Why didn't the Hebrew men obey the king? (**They would bow only to God.**)
4. How did the king punish the three men? (**He threw them into a fiery furnace.**)
5. How did God protect the Hebrew men? (**He sent an angel to protect them.**)

LIFE APPLICATION QUESTION: What things do people worship besides God?
(**Money, cars, jobs, celebrities, and possessions** — *allow for a variety of answers.*)

5. PRAYER FOCUS
Forgiveness for putting things or people ahead of God

REVIEW & MEMORY TIME

REVIEW OPTIONS:
- Bible Basketball
  pg. 107, #6
- Character Quotes
  pg. 108, #8
- Bible Pictionary
  pg. 108, #9
- Balloon Pop Review
  pg. 109, #13

MEMORY VERSE OPTIONS:
- Clothespin Review
  pg. 113, #5
- Clue Word Memory Cards
  pg. 114, #8
- Balloon Pop Race
  pg. 117, #21

MEMORY OBJECT OPTIONS:
- Name That Object
  pg. 119, #4
- Object Sequence
  pg. 119, #5

48 DANIEL

Story Reference: Daniel 6
Memory Verse: Galatians 6:9 — Let us not become weary in doing good, for at the proper time we will reap a harvest if we do not give up.

STORYTELLING TIME

1. TO THE STORYTELLER
BEFORE YOU BEGIN: Ask review questions from the previous ten stories.
Daniel's refusal to bow down to the Babylonian god brings out many themes: prayer, obedience, dedication and service to God. Many of these themes have been covered in previous stories and are worth repeating. But the real key to the story of Daniel is that he takes a strong, unbending stand for God. Children won't necessarily lose their lives for taking a stand, but they could face ridicule. This story shows how God will honor those who take a stand for Him. Now more than ever, we as Christians must take a stand for what we believe. If not, we will lose our distinctiveness in the "cultural blender."

2. STORYTELLING METHODS
A. Story Tape — pg. 67, #1
B. Draw a Picture — pg. 68, #7
C. Bible Time Machine — pg. 69, #12

3. MEMORY OBJECT: A stuffed toy lion
Giveaway: A lion sticker
Story/Object Association: The lions in the den

4. REVIEW QUESTIONS
1. How did King Darius feel about Daniel? (**He liked Daniel.**)
2. What law did King Darius sign? (**That any person who prayed to anyone other than the king would be thrown into the lions' den**)
3. Why didn't Daniel obey the law? (**Because he knew that he should pray only to God**)
4. What was Daniel's punishment for disobeying? (**He was thrown into the lions' den.**)
5. How did God save Daniel? (**God sent an angel to protect him.**)

Life Application Question: How can we stand up for God? (**By telling people that we love God, and by obeying His commands**)

5. PRAYER FOCUS
Courage to take a stand for God this week

REVIEW & MEMORY TIME

REVIEW OPTIONS:
- Overhead Game
  pg. 107, #3
- Bible Basketball
  pg. 107, #6
- Beach Ball Review
  pg. 109, #15
- Story Card Match
  pg. 111, #25

MEMORY VERSE OPTIONS:
- Memory Verse Pocket
  pg. 113, #6
- Chalkboard Verse
  pg. 114, #10
- Memory Verse Sticks
  pg. 117, #20

MEMORY OBJECT OPTIONS:
- Object Match
  pg. 119, #2
- Musical Objects
  pg. 119, #6

ESTHER

49

STORY REFERENCE: Esther 4 – 7
MEMORY VERSE: John 15:13 — Greater love has no one than this, that he lay down his life for his friends.

STORYTELLING TIME

1. TO THE STORYTELLER
BEFORE YOU BEGIN: Ask review questions from the previous ten stories.
Kids will often use the phrase, "I dare you to . . ." Dares usually contain some risk. Doing something because it is risky is okay as long as it is done for the right reason. Esther took a big risk, but for the right reason: to save her people. Her bravery is much like that of those who take action to help others in perilous situations. Bravery is a part of doing what is right and doing it for the right reason.

2. STORYTELLING METHODS
A. Story Tape — pg. 67, #1
B. Storyteller As a Bible Character — pg. 67, #3
C. Floor Map — pg. 68, #5

3. MEMORY OBJECT: A Jumbo pencil
GIVEAWAY: A small pencil
STORY/OBJECT ASSOCIATION: The scepter used by the king to show Esther that she could approach him

4. REVIEW QUESTIONS
1. Who chose Esther to be his queen? **(King Xerxes)**
2. What evil plan did Haman have? **(To kill all of the Jews in his country)**
3. Why was Esther afraid to walk up to the king? **(Because she could be killed if she walked up to him without being called)**
4. What did the king do when Esther walked in? **(He held out his scepter to her.)**
5. What happened to Haman? **(The king had him killed.)**

LIFE APPLICATION QUESTION: When have you had to be brave? *(Allow for various answers.)*

5. PRAYER FOCUS
Bravery to do the right thing when others are in need of help

REVIEW & MEMORY TIME

REVIEW OPTIONS:
- Who Am I?
  pg. 110, #16
- Shaving Cream Review
  pg. 110, #18
- Story Review Cards
  pg. 111, #23
- Change the Bible Story
  pg. 112, #28

MEMORY VERSE OPTIONS:
- Memory Verse Card Drill
  pg. 113, #4
- Pass the Hat
  pg. 114, #9
- Memory Verse Square
  pg. 116, #17

MEMORY OBJECT OPTIONS:
- Bible Biography
  pg. 119, #1
- Name That Object
  pg. 119, #4

63

50 REBUILDING THE WALL

STORY REFERENCE: Nehemiah 4 – 6
MEMORY VERSE: Colossians 3:23 — Whatever you do, work at it with all your heart, as working for the Lord, not for men.

STORYTELLING TIME

1. TO THE STORYTELLER
BEFORE YOU BEGIN: Ask review questions from the previous ten stories.
Whether building a wall, helping to "pick up," or playing together, a spirit of cooperation is vital. We can accomplish a lot more if we work together. It means less work for everyone and encourages real unity. If kids learn the importance of working together, they will be more productive as adult Christians. Some benefits of a positive team initiative are that the experience lingers in the memory longer than solo efforts, unity among the group is established, more is accomplished by a group, and the process instills a desire to do more work for the Lord.

2. STORYTELLING METHODS
A. Story Tape — pg. 67, #1
B. Draw a Picture — pg. 68, #7
C. Narration — pg. 70, #14

3. MEMORY OBJECT: A ruler
Giveaway: A six-inch ruler
Story/Object Association: The rebuilding of the wall of Jerusalem

4. REVIEW QUESTIONS
1. Why was there a wall around Jerusalem? **(To protect the city from enemies)**
2. Why did God let an army destroy Jerusalem? **(Because the Jews did not obey God)**
3. What army took the Jews as prisoners? **(The army of the Babylonians)**
4. Who went to Jerusalem to rebuild the wall? **(Nehemiah)**
5. What did he have each family do? **(Rebuild one portion of the wall)**

Life Application Question: How should Christians work together? **(By helping each other, cooperating, doing projects together** — *allow for a variety of answers.*)

5. PRAYER FOCUS
Seeking God's help to be more cooperative with each other

REVIEW & MEMORY TIME

REVIEW OPTIONS:
- Beach Ball Review
  pg. 109, #15
- Bible Time Capsule
  pg. 110, #21
- Story Card Match
  pg. 111, #25
- Bible Story Bag
  pg. 112, #27

MEMORY VERSE OPTIONS:
- Round Table Memory
  pg. 115, #14
- Balloon Pop Race
  pg. 117, #21
- Name That Verse
  pg. 118, #23

MEMORY OBJECT OPTIONS:
- Object Bag
  pg. 119, #3
- Object Mural
  pg. 120, #8

STORYTELLING AND REVIEW RESOURCES

- Storytelling Methods
- Review Questions and Answers
- Additional Review Questions
- Memory Verse List
- Memory Verse Cards
- Storyteller Memory Object List
- Character Descriptions
- Review Games and Activities
- Memory Verse Games and Activities
- Memory Object Games and Activities
- Charts and Maps

STORYTELLING METHODS

1. Story Tape

Write the story in script form and get a different person for each character in the story. Instead of finding different people for each character, you may be able to create the different voices. Have your story recorded ahead of time so the children can listen to the recording. You will probably want to hold up the memory object while the story is being played. Also, you can have children pantomime the story as the tape is being played.

Many libraries have tapes of different sound effects. This can really enhance a story. Have storm sounds for the story of Noah's ark, trumpets playing for the battle of Jericho, or bird sounds for Elijah being fed by the ravens.

2. Children As Bible Characters

Have children dress up and pretend to be Bible story characters. The children can act out the story as you tell it. (You will need to practice this ahead of time. In order for this to be effective, the children need to know what they should do as you tell the story.) If you have theatrical children who enjoy performing in front of a crowd and do a good job, you may be able to have a few of them act out the story on their own.

3. Storyteller As a Bible Character

You can dress up as a Bible character in the story. Pretend as if you were that person, and give an account of what you have seen or done. Try to stay in character as much as possible. At the end, if you have time, you could let your children ask you questions.

4. Map It Out

This is something that you can do on a weekly basis, or just for certain stories. At some point when you are telling the story, you can point out, on a map, the region you are discussing. You may even want to mark a specific place where the Bible person lived or traveled. You may want to make an overhead transparency of the map, for easier viewing.

5. Floor Map

This is a great storytelling method if the story involves different geographical areas. Designate certain spots in the room to be different geographical places. As you tell the story, whatever area the character is in, stand in that place in the room. When the character moves or travels to another area, walk to that place as you tell the story. You can make this a great review for children. Several times throughout the story, stop and have the children repeat all the places to which the character has traveled.

Variation: Designate children to be characters in the story, and have them walk to the different points on the floor "map" as you tell the story. This really gets the children involved in the story.

6. Seat Performers

Depending on the story, choose a certain hand motion or sound for the children to do each time they hear a key word in the story. For example; in the story of Noah's ark, whenever you mention the word *rain*, the children could hit their hands on their laps repetitively so that it sounds like rain. Younger children might even like to make the different animal noises to imitate the animals on the ark.

7. Draw a Picture

Ask your pastor or youth leader to help you locate a church member or young person with artistic ability. Instead of using the overhead transparency of the Bible Story Card™, have your artist draw the picture on the overhead projector while you are telling the story. You may even want to involve your children a little more by asking them what they think the picture should look like. What expressions would the Bible characters have on their faces? What would the background look like? Then, the children can compare the artist's picture to the Bible Story Card™ to see how the pictures are similar or different.

If you are using this method with a small class, let each child draw a picture of the story on the overhead projector. Have many different colors of overhead markers available. Children love to draw on the overhead projector. If you don't have access to an overhead projector, have different colors of chalk and let each child draw a part of the story on a blackboard. This is also fun.

8. Storytelling Puppet

Don't let this way of telling a story frighten you. You do not need to have an elaborate stage and fancy puppets to tell the story effectively. You can just take a sock and draw two eyes, a nose, and a mouth on it. You will be surprised to see how much the children will watch the puppet (sock) instead of you. If you have the time and the resources, you can dress up the puppet as a particular Bible character and have the puppet tell the story. Remember, whenever you are using more than one puppet, it would help to fluctuate your voice for each puppet. Don't strain your voice! If you do, your pretend "voice" won't sound real. Make your "voices" believable.

9. Spray Can Storytelling

This method of storytelling can be a lot of fun and very successful. Cover a large blackboard with thick, white, paper or an old sheet. Spray paint the story as you tell it, making pictures of the people in your story, or helping the children to learn the geography of the area where the story takes place. This is a great way to review where the people in the Bible were when great events happened, such as when Moses lifted his staff and God parted the Red Sea. What an exciting story! You can show where the Red Sea is by spray painting it on your paper or sheet.

10. Bible Story Apron

Find an apron with many different-sized pockets on it. You may have to sew a few more on. In the pockets, have some objects related to the story. As you tell the story, pull out each appropriate object. For example, lets say you are telling the story of David and Goliath. In one pocket, you may have five smooth stones. In another pocket, you may have a slingshot. In another, you may have small puppets or figures representing David and Goliath. As you tell the story, pull out each of these objects. The nice thing about the apron is that you have a place to put each object when you are ready to show another object. This way of telling a story leaves the children in suspense. They never know what you are going to pull out of your pockets!

11. Bible Story Cards

Before you begin telling the story, give all of the children their Bible Story Card™ for that story. As you tell the story, have the children look at their card. This will help them to associate the characters with the story.

12. Bible Time Machine

Take your children back in time as you tell the Bible story. This may take some preparation, but it will be well worth it. For instance, let's say you are telling the story of Daniel and the lions' den. Bring in a large, brown blanket or tarp, and put it over folding chairs to create the lions' den. You can take paper plates and make lions faces on them to put in the den. This technique helps children to think more carefully about the historical context of the story.

13. SuperCards/Overhead Transparencies

As you tell the story, hold up the Bible story SuperCard™ or have the Bible Story Card™ overhead transparency up so the children can see the picture as you tell the story. This gives them a mental picture of the story characters.

14. Narration

Narration is when a person reads a story with voice inflection and emotion. Be careful when using this method. It can be easy to start reading a story using voice inflections and emotions, but then gradually start to read in a monotone voice. Be enthusiastic and animated, and remember to look up at the children from time to time.

15. TV Story

Decorate a box to look like a television set. Then cut out the section where the television screen would be. On several sheets of paper, draw different scenes of the story. You may want to glue these onto pieces of cardboard or posterboard to make them secure. Have a slot on the top or the side of the television box where you can slide in all of the picture scenes. Put the scenes in order so that as you tell the story, you can pull out each scene in front to show the next scene already in place. It may be beneficial to put tabs on the picture scenes to make them easier to pull out.

REVIEW QUESTIONS & ANSWERS

This entire set of Review Questions & Answers is included on the Memory Verse Cards available from your BibleStoryCards Learning System™ supplier.

1. CREATION
1. How many days did it take to create the world? **(Seven)**
2. What did God use to make Adam? **(The dust of the earth)**
3. What garden did Adam take care of? **(The Garden of Eden)**
4. What did God take from Adam to make Eve? **(One of Adam's ribs)**
5. What other things did God create? **(Plants, trees, water, animals)**

2. THE FIRST SIN
1. Where did Adam and Eve live? **(In the Garden of Eden)**
2. What tree was in the middle of the garden? **(The Tree of the Knowledge of Good and Evil)**
3. What did God tell them about the tree? **(Not to eat the fruit from the tree)**
4. Who tricked Eve into eating the fruit? **(The serpent/Satan)**
5. How did God punish Adam and Eve? **(By making them leave the garden)**

3. CAIN & ABEL
1. Who were the two sons in this story? **(Cain and Abel)**
2. What did Cain bring as an offering to God? **(Crops he had grown)**
3. What did Abel bring as an offering to God? **(The best sheep from his flock)**
4. Why was Cain jealous of Abel? **(Because God accepted Abel's offering, but not Cain's)**
5. What terrible thing did Cain do to Abel? **(He killed Abel.)**

4. NOAH'S ARK
1. Why did God choose Noah to build the ark? **(Because Noah had obeyed God)**
2. Why did God want to destroy all of the people? **(Because they were wicked)**
3. What was Noah supposed to take on the ark? **(Two of every animal)**
4. Who were Noah's three sons? **(Shem, Ham, and Japheth)**
5. Why do people sometimes laugh at God? **(Because they don't love Him)**

5. TOWER OF BABEL
1. When did everyone understand each other? **(In early Bible times)**
2. What did some men decide to build? **(A city and a tower)**
3. How tall did the men want the tower to be? **(Tall enough to reach to the sky)**
4. Why did the men want to build the tower? **(So the people would tell them how great they were)**
5. Why did God mix up the language? **(So the men could not understand each other and would have to stop building the tower)**

6. SODOM & GOMORRAH
1. Where did Lot live? What city was nearby? **(Sodom, Gomorrah)**
2. What were the people like who lived there? **(They were wicked.)**
3. Who did God send to Lot's house? **(Two angels)**
4. What did they tell Lot? **(To leave the city and not look back)**
5. What happened to Lot's wife? Why? **(She turned into a statue of salt because she looked back at the burning cities.)**

7. ABRAHAM OFFERS ISAAC
1. Who was Abraham's son? **(Isaac)**
2. Where did Abraham travel to for the sacrifice? **(Mount Moriah)**
3. What did God tell Abraham to do with his son? **(Sacrifice him)**
4. Why did God test Abraham? **(To see if Abraham would do whatever He asked)**
5. What did God send for Abraham to sacrifice? **(A ram)**

8. JACOB & ESAU
1. Who were Isaac and Rebekah's twin sons? **(Jacob and Esau)**
2. Which son was the oldest? **(Esau)**
3. What special honor did the oldest son receive? **(A birthright)**
4. Why did Esau trade his birthright? **(He wanted a bowl of stew to eat)**
5. Why would Jacob want Esau's birthright? **(So he could be the next leader of his family and receive many of his fathers belongings)**

9. JACOB WRESTLES WITH GOD
1. Who was Jacob traveling home to meet? **(His brother, Esau)**
2. What did Jacob and God do? **(They wrestled.)**
3. What did Jacob want from God? **(A blessing)**
4. Why was God pleased with Jacob? **(Because Jacob wanted a blessing badly enough to fight for it)**
5. What new name did God give to Jacob? **(Israel)**

10. JOSEPH'S COAT
1. Who was Jacob's favorite son? **(Joseph)**
2. What special gift did Jacob make for his son? **(A coat)**
3. Why were Joseph's brothers jealous of him? **(Because their father loved Joseph more than he loved them)**
4. How did Joseph's brothers get rid of him? **(They sold him to slave traders.)**
5. What did Jacob think happened to Joseph? **(An animal killed him.)**

11. JOSEPH IN PRISON
1. Why was Joseph put into prison? **(Because he was accused of a crime, though he did not do it)**
2. Who put Joseph in charge of the prisoners? **(The warden)**
3. What two servants did Pharaoh send to prison? **(The baker and cupbearer)**
4. What did Joseph do for these servants? **(He interpreted their dreams.)**
5. What did Joseph ask the cupbearer to do? **(To ask Pharaoh if he would free Joseph from prison)**

12. JOSEPH RULES IN EGYPT
1. What happened in Pharaoh's dream? **(Seven thin cows ate seven fat cows.)**
2. What servant remembered Joseph from prison? **(The cupbearer)**
3. Who interpreted Pharaoh's dream? **(Joseph)**
4. What did Pharaoh's dream mean? **(That Egypt would have seven good years for raising crops and then seven years of famine)**
5. What was Joseph's job when he became a ruler? **(He was to make sure that there was enough food stored for the seven-year famine.)**

13. BABY MOSES
1. Who did Pharaoh order to be killed? Why? **(Hebrew baby boys; because he thought there were too many Hebrews in his land)**
2. What did Moses' mother do to save him? **(She put him into a basket and placed it in the river.)**
3. Did Moses' mother have faith in God? How? **(Yes; by believing that God would protect her baby while he was in the river)**
4. Who watched the basket float in the river? **(Miriam, Moses' sister)**
5. Who found Moses in the basket? **(Pharaoh's daughter)**

14. THE BURNING BUSH
1. Where did Moses move to after he grew up? **(Midian)**
2. What was different about the bush Moses saw? **(The bush was on fire, but it didn't burn.)**
3. What was Moses supposed to tell Pharaoh? **(To free the Israelites)**
4. How did Moses feel when God spoke to him? **(Afraid)**
5. Why did God say Moses should not be afraid? **(Because God would be with him)**

15. THE PLAGUES
1. Who wanted God to free them from slavery? **(The Israelites)**
2. Who did God send to talk to Pharaoh? **(Moses and Aaron)**
3. What did they tell Pharaoh? **(To free the Israelites)**
4. What happened each time Pharaoh said, "No"? **(God sent a plague to Egypt.)**
5. What were the plagues that God sent to Egypt? **(The waters turned to blood; frogs; gnats; flies; the death of livestock; boils; deadly hail; locusts; and complete darkness)**

16. THE FIRST PASSOVER
1. What was the last plague God sent to Egypt? **(Death of firstborn sons)**
2. When did God say He would pass over Egypt? **(Around midnight)**
3. What instructions did God give to the Israelites? **(Each family was to sacrifice a lamb or a goat, take the blood, and put it on the top and sides of their doorframe.)**
4. What happened to Pharaoh's firstborn son? **(He was killed.)**
5. Why was that night called the "Passover"? **(Because God passed over the homes of the Israelites who obeyed His instructions, and their firstborn sons were not killed)**

17. CROSSING THE RED SEA
1. Why did Pharaoh want the Israelites back? **(He had lost his workers.)**
2. Who led the Israelites out of Egypt? **(Moses)**
3. What sea did the Israelites need to cross? **(The Red Sea)**
4. What did Moses do to make the water roll back? **(He raised his staff and stretched out his hand over the water.)**
5. What happened to the Egyptians who followed? **(They drowned.)**

18. EATING MANNA
1. Why were the Israelites complaining to Moses? **(Because they wanted food to eat)**
2. Why did they wish they had stayed in Egypt? **(Because they had plenty of food to eat in Egypt)**
3. What did God send for the Israelites to eat? **(Manna)**
4. How much were the Israelites told to gather? **(Only enough for each day)**
5. What happened to the extra manna? **(It spoiled)**

19. MOSES STRIKES THE ROCK
1. Why were the Israelites angry? **(Because they didn't have any water to drink)**
2. What was Moses afraid the people would do? **(Kill him)**
3. What did God tell Moses to take with him? **(His walking stick and some of the older leaders)**
4. Where did God say He would be standing? **(In front of Moses by a rock)**
5. How did Moses get water for the Israelites? **(He hit the rock.)**

20. THE TEN COMMANDMENTS
1. What mountain did Moses climb? **(Mount Sinai)**
2. How many rules did God give to Moses? **(Ten)**
3. What are these rules called? **(The Ten Commandments)**
4. What did God write the rules on? **(Stone tablets)**
5. How many rules can you remember? ***(Have the children list the rules.)***

21. THE GOLDEN CALF
1. Who did Moses put in charge of the Israelites? **(Aaron)**
2. Why did the Israelites want a golden idol? **(Because they wanted to worship a god that they could see)**
3. What did the people thank the golden calf for? **(For leading them out of Egypt)**
4. How did the Israelites disobey God? **(They didn't worship Him.)**
5. How did Moses react to the golden calf? **(He was angry and threw the stone tablets with the Ten Commandments onto the ground.)**

22. THE TABERNACLE
1. What did God tell the Israelites to build? **(The Tabernacle)**
2. Why did the Israelites go to the Tabernacle? **(To worship God)**
3. What were the names of the two special rooms? **(The Holy Place and the Most Holy Place)**
4. What hung between the two rooms? **(A curtain)**
5. Where was the ark of the covenant? **(In the Most Holy Place)**

23. TWELVE SPIES
1. How many spies did Moses send into Canaan? **(Twelve)**
2. What were the spies supposed to do in Canaan? **(They were to see what the people and towns were like, and what foods were grown there.)**
3. How many days did the spies explore the land? **(Forty days)**
4. What did the spies carry back from Canaan? **(A large cluster of grapes, pomegranates, and figs)**
5. What report did the spies bring back to Moses? **(Ten of the spies said that the people were too large to fight but Joshua and Caleb wanted to take the land.)**

24. THE BRONZE SNAKE
1. Why did the Israelites wander in the desert? **(Because they believed the bad report from the ten spies, and God did not let them enter the Promised Land)**
2. Why were the Israelites complaining? **(Because they could not enter Canaan)**
3. How did God punish the Israelites? **(He sent poisonous snakes to their camp.)**
4. What did God tell Moses to make? **(A bronze snake to hang on a pole)**
5. How did God use this to help the Israelites? **(He would heal anyone who had been bitten by a snake if the person would look up at the bronze snake.)**

25. BALAAM'S DONKEY
1. Who did the king think would attack Moab? **(The Israelites)**
2. Who did the king send to talk to Balaam? **(The king's messengers)**
3. What did the king want Balaam to do? **(Put a curse on the Israelites)**
4. What did the king offer to give Balaam? **(Money)**
5. How did God get Balaam's attention? **(He made Balaam's donkey talk.)**

26. CROSSING THE JORDAN
1. Who was the Israelites' leader after Moses died? **(Joshua)**
2. Where were the Israelites finally going to enter? **(Canaan/The Promised Land)**
3. What river did the Israelites need to cross? **(The Jordan River)**
4. Who went into the river first? **(The priests)**
5. What happened when they touched the water? **(The river separated.)**

27. FALL OF JERICHO
1. What land did God promise to the Israelites? **(Canaan)**
2. Who already lived in the land? **(The Canaanites)**
3. What was the first city the Israelites conquered? **(Jericho)**
4. What did the Israelites do for six days? **(They marched around the city, one time each day.)**
5. What happened to the city on the seventh day? **(The walls fell down.)**

28. ACHAN
1. What city did the Israelites conquer? **(Jericho)**
2. Why didn't the Israelites win the battle at Ai? **(Because one Israelite disobeyed God and took some valuables from Jericho)**
3. Who took some valuables to keep for himself? **(Achan)**
4. What things did he take? **(Gold, silver, and a robe)**
5. How was he punished for his sin? **(He and his family were stoned to death.)**

29. GIDEON
1. What did God choose Gideon to do? **(Lead an attack on the Midianites)**
2. How many men attacked the Midianite camp? **(Three hundred)**
3. What three things did each man take with him? **(A trumpet, jar, and torch)**
4. How did Gideon defeat the Midianites? **(God helped Gideon's army to scare the Midianites.)**
5. The story of Gideon is found in what book? **(Judges)**

30. SAMSON
1. Who was the woman Samson loved? **(Delilah)**
2. Why did she want Samson to tell her his secret? **(Because the Philistines promised to give her money if she could find out Samson's secret)**
3. What was the secret of Samson's strength? **(The fact that his hair had never been cut)**
4. What did the Philistines do to Samson? **(They gouged out his eyes.)**
5. How did Samson kill the people at the temple? **(He pushed the temple pillars apart and the temple fell to the ground.)**

31. RUTH & NAOMI
1. Who were Naomi's daughters-in-law? **(Ruth and Orpah)**
2. What happened to Naomi's husband and sons? **(They died.)**
3. Where did Naomi beg the women to go? **(Back to their families)**
4. Which daughter-in-law stayed with Naomi? **(Ruth)**
5. What famous king was Ruth's grandson? **(King David)**

32. SAMUEL'S CALL
1. What did Hannah ask God to give her? **(A son)**
2. What did Hannah name her son? **(Samuel)**
3. Where was Samuel taken when he was young? **(To the temple)**
4. Who was really calling to Samuel? **(God)**
5. What jobs did Samuel have when he grew up? **(Prophet, priest, and judge)**

33. SAMUEL ANOINTS SAUL
1. What job did Samuel have for many years? **(Judge of Israel)**
2. What did the Israelites tell Samuel they wanted? **(A king)**
3. Who was chosen to be the first king of Israel? **(Saul)**
4. What did Samuel pour over Saul's head? Why? **(Oil; to show that Saul had been anointed king)**
5. What did Samuel go back and tell the Israelites? **(That God had chosen Saul to be their first king)**

34. SAMUEL ANOINTS DAVID
1. Why could Saul no longer be the king of Israel? **(He disobeyed God)**
2. Why was Samuel supposed to go to Bethlehem? **(To meet Jesse)**
3. How many sons did Jesse have? **(Eight)**
4. Who did God choose to be the new king? **(David)**
5. What did Samuel do to the new king? **(Samuel anointed him with oil.)**

35. DAVID & GOLIATH
1. What was the name of the giant Philistine? **(Goliath)**
2. What did he do to make David angry? **(He said bad things about God's army.)**
3. How tall was the giant? **(Over nine feet tall)**
4. Who killed the giant? **(David)**
5. How did the giant die? **(David threw a stone that hit Goliath in the forehead.)**

36. DAVID SPARES SAUL
1. Why was Saul jealous of David? **(Because David was very successful)**
2. Why did David have to hide from Saul? **(Because Saul was trying to kill him)**
3. Who pulled out a spear to kill Saul? **(Abishai)**
4. What did David take from Saul? **(Saul's spear and water jug)**
5. What did Saul realize the next day? **(That David could have killed him but instead spared his life)**

37. RETURN OF THE ARK
1. Who was the king of Israel before David? **(Saul)**
2. Who had taken the ark from the Israelites? **(The Philistines)**
3. How did David move the ark the first time? **(With a cart)**
4. What was the correct way to move the ark? **(It was to be carried by the poles and never to be touched.)**
5. How did David show that he was happy? **(He danced for joy.)**

38. BUILDING THE TEMPLE
1. Which of David's sons became the new king? **(Solomon)**
2. What did God say the new king would build? **(A temple)**
3. Whom was the Temple specifically built for? **(God)**
4. What didn't the workers do at the building site? **(They did not make any hammering or chiseling noises.)**
5. How was the inside of the Temple decorated? **(Everything was covered in solid gold.)**

39. RAVENS FEED ELIJAH
1. What king did God tell Elijah to go and see? **(King Ahab)**
2. What is a prophet? **(A person who speaks for God)**
3. What message did Elijah give to the king? **(That there would be no rain in the king's land unless Elijah told it to rain)**
4. Where did Elijah hide? **(In a ravine)**
5. How did God provide food for Elijah to eat? **(God had some ravens take food to Elijah.)**

40. FIRE FROM HEAVEN
1. Who did King Ahab worship? **(Baal)**
2. What did Elijah want to prove to King Ahab? **(That Baal was not real)**
3. How did Baal's prophets pray to their god? **(They shouted, danced, and sang.)**
4. What happened when Baal's prophets prayed? **(Nothing)**
5. What happened when Elijah prayed to God? **(God lit the wood on the altar, and the fire consumed the sacrifice and the water in the ditch around the altar.)**

41. NAAMAN

1. What disease did Naaman have? **(Leprosy)**
2. Whom did the servant girl want Naaman to see? **(Elisha, the prophet)**
3. What did the prophet tell Naaman? **(That if Naaman would wash in the Jordan River seven times, he would be cured)**
4. What did Naaman think of this? **(He didn't want to wash in the river because it was muddy and dirty.)**
5. When was Naaman healed from his disease? **(After he washed seven times)**

42. JOASH

1. Why did the evil queen want to kill Joash? **(So that Joash wouldn't become the new king)**
2. Who saved Joash from the queen? **(His aunt)**
3. Where was Joash hidden? **(In the Temple)**
4. What happened to the evil queen? **(She was killed.)**
5. How old was Joash when he was crowned king? **(Seven years old)**

43. JOB

1. What did Satan get permission to do to Job? **(Tempt him)**
2. What was Satan not allowed to do? **(Kill Job)**
3. What things did Satan take away from Job? **(Family, servants, animals)**
4. What did Job's wife want him to do? **(Curse God and die)**
5. How did God bless Job? **(God gave Job back twice as much as he had lost.)**

44. JONAH

1. Where did God ask Jonah to go and preach? **(Nineveh)**
2. Why did Jonah try to run away from God? **(Jonah didn't want to preach to the people at Nineveh.)**
3. What did the crew members do to calm the sea? **(They threw Jonah overboard.)**
4. What happened while Jonah was in the water? **(He was swallowed by a fish.)**
5. What happened when Jonah went to Nineveh? **(All of the people in the city asked God to forgive them of their sins.)**

45. ISAIAH'S VISION

1. What is a vision? **(It is like a dream.)**
2. How did Isaiah describe God's robe? **(Isaiah said the robe was so big that it filled the Temple.)**
3. What is another name for a seraph? **(An angel)**
4. Why did the seraph touch Isaiah's lips? **(The seraph touched Isaiah's lips with the hot piece of coal to show that God wanted to take away Isaiah's sins.)**
5. What did God want Isaiah to go out and do? **(Tell others about God)**

46. JEREMIAH
1. Who was called "the weeping prophet"? **(Jeremiah)**
2. What message did he give to the Israelites? **(That they were not to fight the Babylonian army, because they would lose the fight.)**
3. Why were the king's men angry with Jeremiah? **(They said that Jeremiah didn't want anything good to happen to the Israelites.)**
4. Where did the king's men put Jeremiah? **(Into a cistern)**
5. How did they get Jeremiah out? **(They lowered ropes to him.)**

47. THE FIERY FURNACE
1. Who were the three Hebrew men? **(Shadrach, Meshach, and Abednego)**
2. What did the king order all of the people to do? **(Bow to his statue)**
3. Why didn't the Hebrew men obey the king? **(They would bow only to God.)**
4. How did the king punish the three men? **(He threw them into a fiery furnace.)**
5. How did God protect the Hebrew men? **(He sent an angel to protect them.)**

48. DANIEL
1. How did King Darius feel about Daniel? **(He liked Daniel.)**
2. What law did King Darius sign? **(That any person who prayed to anyone other than the king would be thrown into the lions' den)**
3. Why didn't Daniel obey the law? **(Because he knew that he should pray only to God)**
4. What was Daniel's punishment for disobeying? **(He was thrown into the lions' den.)**
5. How did God save Daniel? **(God sent an angel to protect him.)**

49. ESTHER
1. Who chose Esther to be his queen? **(King Xerxes)**
2. What evil plan did Haman have? **(To kill all of the Jews in his country)**
3. Why was Esther afraid to walk up to the king? **(Because she could be killed if she walked up to him without being called)**
4. What did the king do when Esther walked in? **(He held out his scepter to her.)**
5. What happened to Haman? **(The king had him killed.)**

50. REBUILDING THE WALL
1. Why was there a wall around Jerusalem? **(To protect the city from enemies)**
2. Why did God let an army destroy Jerusalem? **(Because the Jews did not obey God)**
3. What army took the Jews as prisoners? **(The army of the Babylonians)**
4. Who went to Jerusalem to rebuild the wall? **(Nehemiah)**
5. What did he have each family do? **(Rebuild one portion of the wall)**

WHO? REVIEW QUESTIONS • SET 1

This entire set of Review Questions & Answers is available from your BibleStoryCards Learning System™ supplier. Ask for your "Parent Pak Review Resource."

1. Who were the first man and woman created by God? **Adam and Eve**
2. Who disguised himself as a snake to trick Adam and Eve? **Satan**
3. Who killed his brother because God accepted his brother's sacrifice and not his own? **Cain**
4. Who were Noah's three sons? **Shem, Ham, and Japheth**
5. Who stopped the tower of Babel from being built? **God**
6. Who turned into a pillar of salt? **Lot's wife**
7. Who was going to be sacrificed on an altar by his father? **Isaac**
8. Who sold his birthright for a bowl of stew? **Esau**
9. Who wrestled with Jacob? **God**
10. Who had a coat of many colors? **Joseph**
11. Who interpreted dreams for a cupbearer and a baker? **Joseph**
12. Who had a dream about seven thin cows eating seven fat cows? **Pharaoh**
13. Who was put into a basket and placed in a river so he wouldn't be killed? **Moses**
14. Who saw a burning bush? **Moses**
15. Who went with Moses to speak to the pharaoh of Egypt? **Aaron**
16. Who was killed when God passed over each home in Egypt and didn't see any blood on the doorframe? **The oldest son of the family**
17. Who went to Pharaoh and asked him to free the Israelites? **Moses and Aaron**
18. Who complained to Moses because they didn't have much food to eat? **The Israelites**
19. Who told Moses to take his staff and strike the rock so water would come out of it? **God**
20. Who received the Ten Commandments from God? **Moses**
21. Who made an idol from gold for the Israelites to worship? **Aaron**
22. Who was the only person allowed to go into the Most Holy Place of the Tabernacle? **The high priest**
23. Who went to explore the Promised Land for Moses? **The twelve spies**
24. Who were the people that wanted to look at the bronze snake Moses had made? **The Israelites who were bitten by the poisonous snakes**

25. Who owned a donkey that talked to him? **Balaam**

26. Who carried the ark of the covenant into the Jordan River when the river parted? **The priests**

27. Who led the march around the city of Jericho? **Joshua**

28. Who stole some valuables from the city of Jericho and hid them under a rug in his tent? **Achan**

29. Who led three hundred Israelites in an attack on the Midianites? **Gideon**

30. Who tricked Samson into telling his secret about his strength? **Delilah**

31. Who was Ruth's mother-in-law? **Naomi**

32. Who grew up in the temple with Eli, the priest? **Samuel**

33. Who was the first king of Israel? **Saul**

34. Who was Jesse's youngest son who was anointed to be a king of Israel? **David**

35. Who was the giant Philistine that David killed? **Goliath**

36. Who had the chance to kill Saul while he was sleeping, but instead spared his life? **David**

37. Who was anointed the second king of Israel? **David**

38. Who was the man that God said would build a temple for Him? **Solomon**

39. Who was fed by ravens while he was hiding in a ravine? **Elijah**

40. Who told the prophets of Baal that his God was the true God? **Elijah**

41. Who had leprosy and was told to wash in the Jordan River seven times? **Naaman**

42. Who was the boy that became a king when he was very young? **Joash**

43. Who did Satan test by taking away everything he owned and loved? **Job**

44. Who was swallowed by a large fish when he was thrown over the side of a boat? **Jonah**

45. Who had a vision of God sitting on a throne wearing a long robe? **Isaiah**

46. Who was the prophet that was thrown into a cistern? **Jeremiah**

47. Who were the three Hebrew men that were thrown into a fiery furnace? **Shadrach, Meshach, and Abednego**

48. Who was the man that was thrown into a lions' den? **Daniel**

49. Who was the beautiful young Jewish woman that King Xerxes chose to be his queen? **Esther**

50. Who went to Jerusalem to rebuild the wall of the city? **Nehemiah**

WHO? REVIEW QUESTIONS • SET 2

1. Who created the first man and woman? **God**

2. Who did the snake tempt first in Garden of Eden? **Eve**

3. Who was killed by his brother out of jealously over a sacrifice? **Abel**

4. Who was the father of Shem, Ham, and Japheth? **Noah**

5. Who were the people who tried to build a tower that would reach into the heavens? **The people of Babel**

6. Who was the husband of the woman who turned into a pillar of salt? **Lot**

7. Who almost sacrificed his son on an altar? **Abraham**

8. Who bought his brother's birthright with a bowl of stew? **Jacob**

9. Who was the man that God wrestled? **Jacob (Israel)**

10. Who gave Joseph his coat of many colors? **His father, Jacob (Israel)**

11. Who were the prisoners whose dreams Joseph interpreted? **The baker and the cupbearer of the Pharaoh**

12. Who interpreted the pharaoh's dream about the thin and fat cows? **Joseph**

13. Who watched Moses when he was placed in a basket in the river? **His sister, Miriam**

14. Who spoke to Moses from of the burning bush? **God**

15. Who was the brother of Aaron that led the Israelites? **Moses**

16. Who went through Egypt and passed over the houses that had blood on the doorframe? **God**

17. Who kept refusing to free the Israelites from slavery? **Pharaoh**

18. Whom did the Israelites complain to because they didn't have much food to eat? **Moses**

19. Whom did God tell to take his staff and strike a rock so that water would come out of it? **Moses**

20. Who gave Moses the Ten Commandments? **God**

21. Who was angry when the Israelites made an idol from gold? **Moses**

22. Who was the group of people that God told to build a tabernacle for Him? **The Israelites**

23. Who were the two men that gave the "good report" after spying out the Promised Land? **Joshua and Caleb**

24. Who made a bronze snake in order to heal the people? **Moses**

25. Who asked Balaam to put a curse on the Israelites? **The king of Moab**

26. Who walked into the Jordan River carrying the ark of the covenant, causing the waters to part? **The priests**

27. Who were the people that marched around the city of Jericho? **The Israelites**

28. Who discovered that Achan had taken some valuables from Jericho? **Joshua**

29. Whom did Gideon attack with only three hundred soldiers? **The Midianites**

30. Who did Delilah trick into telling the secret of his strength? **Samson**

31. Who was Naomi's daughter-in-law that stayed with her? **Ruth**

32. Whom did Samuel grow up with in the temple? **Eli**

33. Who anointed Saul to be the first king of Israel? **Samuel**

34. Who was David's father? **Jesse**

35. Who killed Goliath, the giant Philistine? **David**

36. Whom did David have a chance to kill, but spared his life? **King Saul**

37. Who were the first two kings of Israel? **Saul and David**

38. Who told David that his son, Solomon, would build a temple? **God**

39. Who was the king that wanted to have Elijah killed? **Ahab**

40. Whom did Elijah have a great contest with on Mount Carmel? **The prophets of Baal**

41. Who told Naaman to wash seven times in the Jordan River? **Elisha**

42. Who wanted to kill Joash so he wouldn't become the new king? **His grandmother, the queen**

43. Who tempted Job by taking away all of his possessions? **Satan**

44. Who were the people that Jonah was supposed to preach to about God? **The people of Nineveh**

45. Who brought a coal to Isaiah and touched his lips? **A seraph (an angel)**

46. Who told the people of Jerusalem that the Babylonian army was going to attack them? **Jeremiah**

47. Who was the king who had Shadrach, Meshach, and Abednego thrown into the fiery furnace? **Nebuchadnezzar**

48. Who was the king who had Daniel thrown into the lions' den? **Darius**

49. Who chose the beautiful Esther to become his queen? **Xerxes**

50. Who was the king who told Nehemiah that he could return to Jerusalem to rebuild the city's wall? **Artaxerxes**

WHAT? REVIEW QUESTIONS

1. What did God take from Adam in order to create Eve? **One of Adam's ribs**
2. What did God forbid Adam and Eve to do? **To eat from the Tree of the Knowledge of Good and Evil**
3. What did Cain bring as a sacrifice to God? **Some grain from his fields**
4. What did God put in the sky to promise that He would never flood the earth again? **A rainbow**
5. What did a group of people try to build that would reach to the sky? **A tower**
6. What twin cities did God burn to the ground because the people were so wicked? **Sodom and Gomorrah**
7. What did God send to Abraham to sacrifice instead of his son? **A ram**
8. What were the names of Isaac's twin sons? **Jacob and Esau**
9. What did Jacob want from the man that wrestled with him? **A blessing**
10. What lie did Joseph's brothers tell their father Jacob? **That their brother was killed by a ferocious animal**
11. What special thing could Joseph do for people when they told him their dreams? **He could tell them what their dreams meant.**
12. What did Joseph tell Pharaoh that his dream about the cows meant? **That there would be seven years of good crops and seven years of famine in Egypt**
13. What river did Moses' mother put the basket into? **The Nile River**
14. What was different about the bush that Moses saw? **The bush was on fire, but it didn't burn up.**
15. What did God turn into blood? **The waters**
16. What was the last plague God sent to Egypt? **The firstborn son of every family would be killed unless God saw the blood on their doorframes.**
17. What sea did God part so the Israelites could escape from the Egyptians? **The Red Sea**
18. What did God send the Israelites to eat when they were in the desert? **Manna**
19. What came out of the rock when Moses hit it with his staff? **Water**
20. What were the tablets made of that Moses brought down from the mountain? **Stone**
21. What was the idol that Aaron made for the Israelites to worship? **A calf**
22. What were the names of the two rooms in the Tabernacle? **The Holy Place and the Most Holy Place**
23. What did the twelve spies bring back to Moses after they had explored the Promised Land? **A cluster of grapes**
24. What poisonous animals did God send into the Israelites' camp? **Snakes**
25. What did Balaam's donkey do that surprised him? **Talked to him**
26. What happened to the Jordan River when the priests stepped into it? **The river separated.**
27. What city did Joshua march around seven times? **Jericho**
28. What three valuables did Achan steal from Jericho? **Gold, silver, and a robe**

29. What three things did Gideon give his men to take with them on the attack of the Midianites? **A trumpet, a jar, and a torch**

30. What was the secret to Samson's strength? **If he ever cut his hair, he would lose his strength.**

31. What were the names of Naomi's two daughters-in-law? **Ruth and Orpah**

32. What did Eli tell Samuel to say the next time he heard God calling to him? **"Speak, Lord, for your servant is listening."**

33. What did Samuel pour over Saul's head when he anointed him? **Oil**

34. What job did David have before he became the second king of Israel? **He was a shepherd.**

35. What did David use to kill Goliath? **A slingshot and a small stone**

36. What did David and his friend, Abishai, take from Saul while he was sleeping? **Saul's water jug and spear**

37. What special thing did King David want to bring back to Jerusalem and put back in the Temple? **The ark of the covenant**

38. What did the inside of the temple that Solomon built look like? **Everything inside was made of gold.**

39. What types of things did the ravens take to Elijah for him to eat? **Meat and bread**

40. What happened when Elijah prayed and asked God to start a fire and light the wood on the altar? **God sent a fire that burned up the sacrifice, the altar, and the water in the ditch around the altar.**

41. What terrible disease did Naaman have? **Leprosy**

42. What did Joash's aunt do to save him? **She took baby Joash and his nurse to the Temple so his grandmother wouldn't find him.**

43. What tests did Satan give to Job? **Satan took away Job's wealth and his children, and he covered Job's body with sores.**

44. What did Jonah do after the large fish spit him onto the shore? **He went to Nineveh to preach to the people about God.**

45. What were the seraphs like that Isaiah saw in his vision? **Angels**

46. What did Jeremiah tell the people in Jerusalem that made the king's men so angry? **He told the Israelite people not to fight the Babylonian army because they were going to lose.**

47. What did King Nebuchadnezzar see when he looked into the fiery furnace to check on the Hebrew men? **He saw another man in the furnace with the three Hebrew men.**

48. What law did Daniel break that caused him to be put into the lions' den? **The law which said that the people could pray only to the king's god**

49. What did King Xerxes do with his scepter to show Queen Esther that she wouldn't be killed? **He lowered it to Queen Esther for her to touch.**

50. What other name did the Jews have for the city of Jerusalem? **The Holy City**

WHERE? REVIEW QUESTIONS

1. Where did Adam and Eve live? **In the Garden of Eden**

2. Where was the Tree of the Knowledge of Good and Evil located in the Garden of Eden? **In the middle of the garden**

3. Where did Cain take his brother to kill him? **To a field**

4. Where did Noah take his family and two of every kind of animal? **Onto the ark**

5. Where did the people of Babel want their tower to reach? **To the sky**

6. Where did Lot and his family live? **In Sodom**

7. Where did Abraham take Isaac to sacrifice him? **To Mount Moriah**

8. Where had Esau been when he came home tired and hungry? **Out hunting**

9. Where did the man who was wrestling with Jacob touch and injure him? **On his hip**

10. Where did Joseph's brothers put him before they sold him? **Into a well**

11. Where was Joseph taken after he was sold into slavery? **To Egypt**

12. Where was the terrible famine that lasted seven years? **In Egypt**

13. Where did Moses grow up? **In Egypt**

14. Where were the Israelites when Moses freed them from slavery? **In Egypt**

15. Where did Moses and Aaron go to talk to Pharaoh about freeing the Israelites? **To Egypt**

16. Where were the people supposed to put the blood of the animal for the Passover? **On the top and sides of the doorframe**

17. Where were the Egyptians when the water from this sea caved in on them? **In the Red Sea**

18. Where were the Israelites wandering when God sent manna for them to eat? **In the desert**

19. Where was Moses when he struck a rock and water came out of it? **Mount Sinai**

20. Where did Moses go to get the Ten Commandments from God? **Mount Sinai**

21. Where was Moses when Aaron made the golden calf? **On Mount Sinai receiving the Ten Commandments from God**

22. Where did the Israelites worship that had two rooms separated by a beautiful curtain? **At the Tabernacle**

23. Where did Moses send the twelve spies? **Into Canaan, the Promised Land**

24. Where did the Israelites have to look so they wouldn't die from their snakebites? **At the bronze snake that God had told Moses to make**

25. Where was Balaam going when his donkey started talking to him? **To Moab to see the king**

26. Where was the Promised Land the Israelites were going to when they were stopped by the Jordan River? **In Canaan**

27. Where were the Israelites when they marched around the city seven times and the walls fell to the ground? **At Jericho**

28. Where did Achan hide the valuables he stole from Jericho? **In a hole, under a rug in his tent**

29. Where did God tell Gideon and his army to go and attack this large army? **To the Midianite's camp**

30. Where was Samson when he pushed the pillars apart and everything crumbled to the ground? **At the Philistine temple**

31. Where did Orpah go when she left Naomi and Ruth? **Back to her family**

32. Where did Samuel and Eli live? **In the temple**

33. Where did Samuel pour the oil when he anointed Saul? **On Saul's head**

34. Where did David live before he became the King of Israel? **In Bethlehem**

35. Where did David hit Goliath with the stone? **In the forehead**

36. Where were Saul's water jug and spear laying when David and Abishai took them? **By his head**

37. Where did God say that it would be safe to touch the ark of the covenant and not be killed? **On the handles of the ark**

38. Where would most of the Israelites stand when they worshiped at the Temple? **Outside**

39. Where was Elijah hiding when God sent some ravens to feed him? **In a ravine**

40. Where did Elijah dig a ditch when he was challenging the prophets of Baal? **Around his altar to God**

41. Where was Naaman supposed to bathe so that he could be cured of his leprosy? **In the Jordan River**

42. Where was baby Joash hidden so that his grandmother, the queen, wouldn't kill him? **In the Temple**

43. Where was Job sitting when he scraped his sores with a piece of broken pottery? **On a pile of ashes**

44. Where did God ask Jonah to go and preach, but Jonah didn't want to go? **To Nineveh**

45. Where did the seraph touch Isaiah with the hot coal? **On his lips**

46. Where did the king's men put Jeremiah after they heard him tell the Jews that they would lose their fight? **Into a cistern**

47. Where were Shadrach, Meshach, and Abednego thrown because they didn't worship the golden statue? **Into a fiery furnace**

48. Where was Daniel thrown because he prayed to God? **Into a lions' den**

49. Where did Queen Esther walk that put her in a lot of danger? **Into the king's court without being called**

50. Where did Nehemiah go to rebuild the wall of this city? **To Jerusalem**

WHY? REVIEW QUESTIONS

1. Why did God create Adam and Eve? **God would have companionship.**
2. Why did Eve decide to eat the forbidden fruit? **Eve thought that she would become wise, like God.**
3. Why was Cain so jealous of his brother, Abel? **God accepted Abel's sacrifice and not Cain's.**
4. Why did God choose Noah to build the ark and to be saved from the flood? **Noah was good man and blameless in God's sight.**
5. Why was the tower of Babel given its name? **When God mixed up the languages, the people couldn't understand each other.**
6. Why were Lot and his family told to leave Sodom? **God was going to have Sodom and Gomorrah destroyed.**
7. Why did God ask Abraham to sacrifice his son? **God was testing Abraham to see if he would obey.**
8. Why was Esau supposed to receive the birthright from his father, Isaac? **Esau was the oldest son.**
9. Why did God bless Jacob and change his name? **Jacob wanted a blessing badly enough that he was willing to fight for it.**
10. Why did Joseph's brothers hate him so much? **The brothers were jealous of Joseph because he was their father's favorite son.**
11. Why did the warden of the jail put Joseph in charge of the other prisoners? **The warden trusted Joseph.**
12. Why did Joseph have the Egyptians store up food for seven years? **Joseph knew that there would be a terrible famine in Egypt.**
13. Why did Moses' mother have to hide him? **Pharaoh ordered that all of the Hebrew baby boys were to be killed.**
14. Why did God tell Moses to go to Egypt and talk to Pharaoh? **God wanted Moses to tell Pharaoh to free the Israelites.**
15. Why did God send plagues to Egypt? **Pharaoh wouldn't free the Israelites from slavery.**
16. Why was Pharaoh's oldest son killed when God passed over Egypt? **Pharaoh refused to free the Israelites from slavery.**
17. Why did Pharaoh finally listen to Moses and let the Israelites go free? **Pharaoh knew that God was real when his oldest son was killed by the angel of death.**
18. Why did the Israelites only gather enough manna to use for that day? **If the Israelites gathered more, it would spoil before the next day.**
19. Why did Moses strike the rock at Mount Sinai? **God told Moses that if he would strike the rock with his staff, water would come out of it for the Israelites to drink.**
20. Why did God give Moses the Ten Commandments for the Israelites? **God wanted the Israelites to have rules to follow.**
21. Why did the Israelites want an idol to worship? **The Israelites wanted a god that they could see.**
22. Why didn't the Israelites go into the Most Holy Place of the Tabernacle? **Only the high priest could go into the Most Holy Place of the Tabernacle.**
23. Why did Moses send spies into the Promised Land? **Moses wanted them to explore the Promised Land.**
24. Why did some of the Israelites look at the bronze snake that God told Moses to make? **That was the only way those bitten by the snakes would be saved from death.**
25. Why did God make Balaam's donkey talk to him? **God needed to get Balaam's attention to tell him not to go to Moab.**
26. Why couldn't the Israelites cross the Jordan River on their way to the promised land? **The river was flooded and could not be crossed easily.**
27. Why did Joshua and the Israelites march around the city of Jericho seven times? **God told the Israelites that if they would do this, the walls of the city would fall.**

28. Why was Achan put to death? **Achan disobeyed God and took some valuables from the city of Jericho.**
29. Why did the Midianites end up killing each other when Gideon's army attacked them? **The Midianites were so confused by all of the noise that they didn't know who they were killing.**
30. Why did Samson ask God to give him strength one last time? **Samson was in the Philistine temple and wanted to push the two main pillars apart so the temple would fall.**
31. Why did Ruth stay with Naomi instead of going back to her family? **Ruth loved Naomi so much that she didn't want to leave her.**
32. Why did Hannah take her son, Samuel, to live in the temple with Eli, the priest? **Hannah had promised God that if He would give her a son, she would give her son back to God.**
33. Why did the Israelites want a king instead of a priest? **All of the countries around Israel had kings, so they wanted a king also.**
34. Why did Samuel go to Bethlehem to talk to Jesse? **Samuel knew that one of Jesse's sons would be the next king of Israel.**
35. Why were the Israelites afraid of Goliath and the Philistines? **The Philistines were known for being very large men. Goliath was the largest of all the Philistines.**
36. Why did David have to hide from Saul? **Saul kept trying to kill David.**
37. Why did Uzzah die when he touched the ark of the covenant? **Uzzah touched a part of the ark that God said not to touch.**
38. Why did Solomon not want any tools to be used at the building site while the Temple was being built? **Solomon wanted to show respect to God by not having any loud noises at the building site.**
39. Why did Elijah have to be fed by the ravens? **Elijah was hiding and did not want to wander out and possibly be seen.**
40. Why did Elijah want God to light the wood on his altar? **Elijah wanted the prophets of Baal to know that his God was the only true God.**
41. Why did Naaman not want to wash in the Jordan River like Elisha told him to? **The Jordan River was very dirty.**
42. Why did Joash's grandmother have all of the royal family killed? **Joash's grandmother wanted to be the queen.**
43. Why did Satan want to test Job? **Satan wanted to see if Job worshiped God only because God had given him so much.**
44. Why did the men on Jonah's boat throw him into the sea? **Jonah told them that it was the only way for the sea to calm down.**
45. Why did God ask Isaiah, "Whom shall I send?" **God wanted Isaiah to say that he would go and tell others about God.**
46. Why did the king have Jeremiah thrown into a cistern? **Jeremiah told his soldiers that they were not going to win the fight against the Babylonians.**
47. Why were the three Hebrew men thrown into the fiery furnace? **The Hebrew men would not bow down and worship the idol.**
48. Why was Daniel thrown into the lions' den? **King Darius ordered that everyone must pray to his statue, and Daniel disobeyed the king's order.**
49. Why were people surprised to see Queen Esther go to see the king without being called? **No one was supposed to go to the king unless the king called that person. Esther could have been killed.**
50. Why did some men have to guard the city of Jerusalem while other men were rebuilding the city's wall? **Some men said that they would attack while the men were rebuilding the wall of Jerusalem.**

This entire set of Review Questions & Answers is available from your BibleStoryCards Learning System™ supplier. Ask for your "Parent Pak Review Resource."

OLD TESTAMENT MEMORY VERSE LIST

1. **Genesis 1:1** — In the beginning God created the heavens and the earth.
2. **1 John 1:9** — If we confess our sins, he is faithful and just and will forgive us our sins and purify us from all unrighteousness.
3. **Galatians 5:26** — Let us not become conceited, provoking and envying each other.
4. **Genesis 6:8** — But Noah found favor in the eyes of the Lord.
5. **Proverbs 16:18** — Pride goes before destruction, a haughty spirit before a fall.
6. **2 Corinthians 6:14a** — Do not be yoked with unbelievers. For what do righteousness and wickedness have in common?
7. **Genesis 22:18** — And through your offspring all nations on earth will be blessed, because you have obeyed me.
8. **1 Thessalonians 5:21** — Test everything. Hold on to the good.
9. **Genesis 32:28** — Then the man said, "Your name will no longer be Jacob, but Israel, because you have struggled with God and with men and have overcome."
10. **Ephesians 4:32a** — Be kind and compassionate to one another.
11. **Genesis 39:20b-21a** — But while Joseph was there in the prison, the Lord was with him.
12. **Romans 8:28** — And we know that in all things God works for the good of those who love him, who have been called according to his purpose.
13. **Psalm 91:2** — I will say of the Lord, "He is my refuge and my fortress, my God, in whom I trust."
14. **Exodus 3:2** — There the angel of the Lord appeared to him in flames of fire from within a bush. Moses saw that though the bush was on fire it did not burn up.
15. **Jeremiah 33:3** — Call to me and I will answer you and tell you great and unsearchable things you do not know.
16. **1 John 1:7b** — And the blood of Jesus, his Son, purifies us from all sin.
17. **Exodus 14:14** — The Lord will fight for you; you need only to be still.
18. **John 6:33** — For the bread of God is he who comes down from heaven and gives life to the world.
19. **Philippians 2:14** — Do everything without complaining or arguing.
20. **Deuteronomy 6:17a** — Be sure to keep the commands of the Lord your God.
21. **Exodus 20:3** — You shall have no other gods before me.
22. **Exodus 25:8** — Then have them make a sanctuary for me, and I will dwell among them.
23. **Psalm 56:3** — When I am afraid, I will trust in you.
24. **Proverbs 3:5** — Trust in the Lord with all your heart and lean not on your own understanding.
25. **Hebrews 3:15** — Today, if you hear his voice, do not harden your hearts as you did in the rebellion.
26. **Hebrews 10:23** — Let us hold unswervingly to the hope we profess, for he who promised is faithful.
27. **Hebrews 11:30** — By faith the walls of Jericho fell, after the people had marched around them for seven days.

28. **Romans 6:23** — For the wages of sin is death, but the gift of God is eternal life in Christ Jesus our Lord.
29. **1 Corinthians 1:27** — But God chose the foolish things of the world to shame the wise; God chose the weak things of the world to shame the strong.
30. **Ephesians 6:10** — Finally, be strong in the Lord and in his mighty power.
31. **Ruth 1:16** — But Ruth replied, "Don't urge me to leave you or to turn back from you. Where you go I will go, and where you stay I will stay. Your people will be my people and your God my God."
32. **Jeremiah 29:11** — "For I know the plans I have for you," declares the Lord, "plans to prosper you and not to harm you, plans to give you hope and a future."
33. **John 15:19b** — As it is, you do not belong to the world, but I have chosen you out of the world.
34. **1 Samuel 15:22a** — Does the Lord delight in burnt offerings and sacrifices as much as in obeying the voice of the Lord?
35. **John 17:15** — My prayer is not that you take them out of the world but that you protect them from the evil one.
36. **Romans 12:17** — Do not repay anyone evil for evil. Be careful to do what is right in the eyes of everybody.
37. **John 14:23a** — Jesus replied, "If anyone loves me, he will obey my teaching."
38. **John 4:24** — God is spirit, and his worshipers must worship in spirit and in truth.
39. **Philippians 4:19** — And my God will meet all your needs according to his glorious riches in Christ Jesus.
40. **Matthew 7:7** — Ask and it will be given to you; seek and you will find; knock and the door will be opened to you.
41. **James 4:10** — Humble yourselves before the Lord, and he will lift you up.
42. **Isaiah 11:6b** — And a little child will lead them.
43. **1 Corinthians 10:13** — And God is faithful; he will not let you be tempted beyond what you can bear.
44. **Jonah 1:3a** — But Jonah ran away from the Lord and headed for Tarshish.
45. **Isaiah 6:8** — Then I heard the voice of the Lord saying, "Whom shall I send? And who will go for us?" And I said, "Here am I. Send me!"
46. **Psalm 40:2** — He lifted me out of the slimy pit, out of the mud and mire; he set my feet on a rock and gave me a firm place to stand.
47. **Mark 12:30** — Love the Lord your God with all your heart and with all your soul and with all your mind and with all your strength.
48. **Galatians 6:9** — Let us not become weary in doing good, for at the proper time we will reap a harvest if we do not give up.
49. **John 15:13** — Greater love has no one than this, that he lay down his life for his friends.
50. **Colossians 3:23** — Whatever you do, work at it with all your heart, as working for the Lord, not for men.

OLD TESTAMENT MEMORY VERSE CARDS

Teacher Pak Review Resource

This entire set of 3" x 5" Memory Verse Cards is available from your BibleStoryCards Learning System™ supplier.

CREATION — 1.

In the beginning God created the heavens and the earth.
Genesis 1:1

THE FIRST SIN — 2.

If we confess our sins, he is faithful and just and will forgive us our sins and purify us from all unrighteousness.
1 John 1:9

CAIN & ABEL — 3.

Let us not become conceited, provoking and envying each other.
Galatians 5:26

NOAH'S ARK — 4.

But Noah found favor in the eyes of the LORD.
Genesis 6:8

TOWER OF BABEL — 5.

Pride goes before destruction, a haughty spirit before a fall.
Proverbs 16:18

SODOM & GOMORRAH — 6.

Do not be yoked together with unbelievers. For what do righteousness and wickedness have in common?
2 Corinthians 6:14a

ABRAHAM OFFERS ISAAC 7.

And through your offspring all nations
on earth will be blessed,
because you have obeyed me.
Genesis 22:18

JACOB & ESAU 8.

Test everything. Hold on to the good.
1 Thessalonians 5:21

JACOB WRESTLES WITH GOD 9.

Then the man said, "Your name will no
longer be Jacob, but Israel, because
you have struggled with God and with
men and have overcome."
Genesis 32:28

JOSEPH'S COAT 10.

Be kind and compassionate to
one another.
Ephesians 4:32a

JOSEPH IN PRISON 11.

But while Joseph was there in the
prison, the LORD was with him.
Genesis 39:20b-21a

JOSEPH RULES IN EGYPT 12.

And we know that in all things God works
for the good of those who love him, who
have been called according to his purpose.
Romans 8:28

BABY MOSES 13.

I will say of the LORD, "He is my
refuge and my fortress, my God, in
whom I trust."
Psalm 91:2

THE BURNING BUSH 14.

There the angel of the LORD appeared to
him in flames of fire from within a bush.
Moses saw that though the bush was
on fire it did not burn up.
Exodus 3:2

THE PLAGUES 15.

Call to me and I will answer you
and tell you great and unsearchable
things you do not know.
Jeremiah 33:3

THE FIRST PASSOVER 16.

And the blood of Jesus, his Son,
purifies us from all sin.
1 John 1:7b

CROSSING THE RED SEA — 17.

The Lord will fight for you;
you need only to be still.
Exodus 14:14

EATING MANNA — 18.

For the bread of God is he who
comes down from heaven and
gives life to the world.
John 6:33

MOSES STRIKES THE ROCK — 19.

Do everything without
complaining or arguing.
Philippians 2:14

THE TEN COMMANDMENTS — 20.

Be sure to keep the commands of
the Lord your God.
Deuteronomy 6:17a

THE GOLDEN CALF — 21.

You shall have no other
gods before me.
Exodus 20:3

THE TABERNACLE — 22.

Then have them make a sanctuary for me,
and I will dwell among them.
Exodus 25:8

TWELVE SPIES — 23.

When I am afraid, I will trust in you.
Psalm 56:3

THE BRONZE SNAKE — 24.

Trust in the Lord with all your heart and
lean not on your own understanding.
Proverbs 3:5

BALAAM'S DONKEY — 25.

Today, if you hear his voice,
do not harden your hearts as you
did in the rebellion.
Hebrews 3:15

CROSSING JORDAN — 26.

Let us hold unswervingly to the hope we
profess, for he who promised is faithful.
Hebrews 10:23

FALL OF JERICHO — 27.

By faith the walls of Jericho fell, after the people had marched around them for seven days.

Hebrews 11:30

ACHAN — 28.

For the wages of sin is death, but the gift of God is eternal life in Christ Jesus our Lord.

Romans 6:23

GIDEON — 29.

But God chose the foolish things of the world to shame the wise; God chose the weak things of the world to shame the strong.

1 Corinthians 1:27

SAMSON — 30.

Finally, be strong in the Lord and in his mighty power.

Ephesians 6:10

RUTH & NAOMI — 31.

But Ruth replied, "Don't urge me to leave you or to turn back from you. Where you go I will go, and where you stay I will stay. Your people will be my people and your God my God."

Ruth 1:16

SAMUEL'S CALL — 32.

"For I know the plans I have for you," declares the LORD, "plans to prosper you and not to harm you, plans to give you hope and a future."

Jeremiah 29:11

SAMUEL ANOINTS SAUL — 33.

As it is, you do not belong to the world, but I have chosen you out of the world.

John 15:19b

SAMUEL ANOINTS DAVID — 34.

Does the LORD delight in burnt offerings and sacrifices as much as in obeying the voice of the LORD?

1 Samuel 15:22a

DAVID & GOLIATH — 35.

My prayer is not that you take them out of the world but that you protect them from the evil one.

John 17:15

DAVID SPARES SAUL — 36.

Do not repay anyone evil for evil. Be careful to do what is right in the eyes of everybody.

Romans 12:17

RETURN OF THE ARK — 37.

Jesus replied, "If anyone loves me,
he will obey my teaching."
John 14:23a

BUILDING THE TEMPLE — 38.

God is spirit, and his worshipers must
worship in spirit and in truth.
John 4:24

RAVENS FEED ELIJAH — 39.

And my God will meet all your needs
according to his glorious riches
in Christ Jesus.
Philippians 4:19

FIRE FROM HEAVEN — 40.

Ask and it will be given to you;
seek and you will find; knock and the
door will be opened to you.
Matthew 7:7

NAAMAN — 41.

Humble yourselves before the Lord,
and he will lift you up.
James 4:10

JOASH — 42.

And a little child will lead them.
Isaiah 11:6b

JOB — 43.

And God is faithful; he will not let you
be tempted beyond what you can bear.
1 Corinthians 10:13

JONAH — 44.

But Jonah ran away from the LORD and
headed for Tarshish.
Jonah 1:3a

ISAIAH'S VISION — 45.

Then I heard the voice of the Lord
saying, "Whom shall I send?
And who will go for us?" And I said,
"Here am I. Send me!"
Isaiah 6:8

JEREMIAH — 46.

He lifted me out of the slimy pit, out of
the mud and mire; he set my feet on a
rock and gave me a firm place to stand.
Psalm 40:2

THE FIERY FURNACE — 47.

Love the Lord your God with all your heart and with all your soul and with all your mind and with all your strength.

Mark 12:30

DANIEL — 48.

Let us not become weary in doing good, for at the proper time we will reap a harvest if we do not give up.

Galatians 6:9

ESTHER — 49.

Greater love has no one than this, that he lay down his life for his friends.

John 15:13

REBUILDING THE WALL — 50.

Whatever you do, work at it with all your heart, as working for the Lord, not for men.

Colossians 3:23

STORYTELLER MEMORY OBJECT LIST PAGE

The first item listed by each number is the object to be used when telling the story.
The second item listed is the suggested give away object.

This entire set of Review Questions & Answers is available from your
BibleStoryCards Learning System™ supplier. Request the "Memory Object Box."

1. A leaf
   A leaf

2. A piece of fruit
   A small apple

3. A Shredded Wheat box
   A sugar-coated shredded wheat square

4. Animal Crackers or a toy boat
   An animal cracker

5. Legos
   Sand-colored sponges cut into rectangular pieces

6. A Morton's Salt container
   A restaurant-size salt packet

7. A rubber knife
   A small plastic knife

8. A can of beans or soup
   A dried bean

9. A name tag
   A name tag for each child

10. A brightly colored coat/robe or swatch of cloth
    A piece of brightly colored cloth

11. A key
    A small key

12. An oatmeal container
    A small bag of oatmeal

13. A doll, basket or cattail
    A small, plastic baby doll

14. A small bush or plant
    A branch from a bush

15. A frog (plastic or real)
    A frog sticker

16. A toy lamb or bag of cotton balls
    A white cotton ball

17. A large stick or staff
    A short piece of a dowel rod

18. Necco Wafers or other cookies
    A Necco Wafer

19. A water bottle
    A small rock

20. A scroll
    A scroll with the Ten Commandments written on it

21. A bracelet or toy cow
    A friendship bracelet

22. A piece of canvas-colored cloth
    A small piece of canvas-colored cloth

23. Grapes or Fig Newtons
    Grapes

24. A toy snake
    A Gummy Worm

25. A toy donkey
    A toy donkey

26. Sandals
    A sandal key chain

27. **A trumpet**
    A party horn or kazoo

28. **A candy coin wrapped in foil** or play money
    A candy coin wrapped in gold foil

29. **A large candle**
    A small candle

30. **A pair of scissors**
    A pair of children's scissors

31. **A map** or airline baggage tag
    A map

32. **A telephone** or pillow
    A Whatchama*call*it candy bar

33. **A Head and Shoulders shampoo bottle**
    A trial-size bottle of shampoo

34. **A bottle of baby oil** or a can of motor oil
    A trial-size bottle of baby oil or lotion

35. **A slingshot**
    A small, round stone or a slingshot

36. **A spear**
    A piece of *spear*mint gum

37. **A jewelry box** or a treasure chest
    A small treasure chest

38. **A sponge "brick"**
    A red sponge

39. **Oyster crackers**
    A few oyster crackers

40. **Caramel candies**
    A piece of caramel candy

41. **A bar of soap**
    A hotel-sized bar of soap

42. **A Burger King crown**
    A Burger King crown

43. **A box of bandage strips**
    A bandage strip

44. **A box of fish crackers**
    A few fish crackers

45. **A piece of charcoal**
    A pair of waxed lips

46. **A rope**
    A piece of yarn or string

47. **A box of matches**
    A piece of cinnamon or fireball candy

48. **A stuffed toy lion**
    A lion sticker

49. **A Jumbo pencil**
    A small pencil

50. **A ruler**
    A six-inch ruler

This entire set of Storyteller Memory Objects is available from your BibleStoryCards Learning System™ supplier. Request the "Memory Object Box."

BibleStoryCards™

OT CHARACTER DESCRIPTIONS

AARON — He was the younger brother of Moses and the first high priest of Israel. Aaron was appointed temporary judge of the Israelites while Moses was on Mount Sinai, and he built an idol of gold while Moses went up to Mount Sinai to receive the Ten Commandments.

ABEDNEGO — This Hebrew man, along with two others, Shadrach and Meshach, was thrown into a fiery furnace for not bowing down to the idol of the Babylonian king, Nebuchadnezzar.

ABEL — He was the second son of Adam and Eve. Abel and his brother, Cain, each gave sacrifices to God. God accepted Abel's sacrifice and not Cain's. Cain's jealousy led him to murder Abel.

ABISHAI — He was David's nephew and loyal friend. David stopped Abishai from killing King Saul as he slept.

ABRAHAM — He was called the father of the people of God. Abraham and his wife, Sarah, were given a son, Isaac, in their old age. Abraham was asked by God to sacrifice his son, but God intervened.

ACHAN — After the Israelites defeated the city of Jericho, Achan deliberately disobeyed God's orders and stole some goods from the city to keep for himself. He and his family were later killed for his actions.

ADAM — He was the first man created by God. He and his wife, Eve, were placed in the Garden of Eden to live obediently for God. When they fell to temptation, a sinful pattern was set for all of humanity.

AHAB (KING) — Ahab was the seventh king of Israel. While he was king, he promoted Baal worship. It was while he was king that Elijah challenged the prophets of Baal.

BAAL — This was a fertility and nature god worshiped by many people. The prophet Elijah challenged the prophets of Baal to see which god would light a fire on his altar.

BABYLONIANS — These were people who lived in the region directly north of Arabia. The Babylonians conquered and took captive the people of Judah.

BALAAM — The king of Moab sent messengers to ask Balaam to put a curse on the Israelites. As Balaam was traveling to Moab to give the king his response, God caused the donkey Balaam was riding on to speak to Balaam in order to make sure he told the Moabites only what God wanted him to say.

BEZALEL — He was a craftsman who helped to complete the building and decorating of the Tabernacle.

BOAZ — He was a wealthy landowner who married a widowed Moabite woman, Ruth, who was working in his fields. Boaz was the great-grandfather of King David.

Cain — The oldest son of Adam and Eve. He was the first person to murder another man — his brother, Abel. During Cain's time of wandering, he built the first city, Enoch.

Caleb — He was one of the twelve spies who was sent into Canaan to scout the Promised Land. Caleb and Joshua were the only two who believed that God could help them conquer the land. Also, they were the only two of the spies who were allowed to enter the Promised Land.

Canaanites — These people occupied the land of Canaan before the Israelites took over. The Canaanites are the descendants of Ham, one of Noah's sons.

Daniel — This great prophet continued to pray to God instead of the king, and was thrown into a den of lions. Because of his faith, God closed the mouths of the lions and Daniel's life was spared.

Darius (King) — He was a king of the Persian Empire. While he was king, the Jews rebuilt the Temple in Jerusalem. This Temple replaced the one that the Babylonians had destroyed many years earlier. Darius contributed financially to this project.

David — This young shepherd boy was chosen by God to be the second king of Israel. David had a deep trust and respect for God. Many of his prayers are found in the book of Psalms.

Delilah — She was a Philistine woman who was bribed by the Philistine government to trick Samson into telling the secret of his strength.

Egyptians — These were people of Egypt who held the Israelites in captivity for 430 years.

Eli — He was a high priest of Israel who also served as a judge. Eli took young Samuel into the temple and taught him the ways of God.

Elijah — He is considered the greatest prophet of the Old Testament. He spoke against the prophets of Baal and challenged them on Mount Carmel. He then hid in a ravine, fearing for his life. God provided for him by sending ravens to bring food to him.

Elisha — This prophet of Israel was a great miracle worker and was the successor to the prophet Elijah. He was concerned about the justice and morality in his nation and became an advisor to the kings.

Esau — The oldest of Isaac and Rebekah's twin sons, Esau was called "the hairy one," and his nickname was "Red" because of his red hair color. He disregarded the value of his birthright and sold the birthright to his twin brother, Jacob, for a bowl of stew.

Esther — She was an orphaned Jewish girl chosen by King Xerxes to be his queen. Esther discovered that the king's prime minister, Haman, was trying to kill all of the Jews. Knowing her life was in danger, Esther approached the king to tell him of Haman's evil plan. By doing this, she saved her people.

Eve — The first woman created by God, Eve is called the mother of all men. The sin that Eve and her husband, Adam, committed produced a sinful nature in all mankind.

Gideon — This man was chosen by God to lead a small army of 300 men on an attack of the Midianites, who were successfully defeated. For forty years Gideon served as a judge over Israel.

Goliath — This Philistine giant stood over nine feet tall. When he mocked God and the Israelite army, the young David bravely approached him. With a slingshot and a small stone, David struck Goliath in the forehead and killed him.

Ham — He was the youngest son of Noah. Ham and his wife accompanied his father, Noah, on the ark during the Flood. It is believed that Ham's descendants eventually became the Canaanites.

Haman — He was a prime minister of Persia who plotted to kill all of the Jews because Mordecai, a Jew, refused to bow down to him. When Queen Esther told King Xerxes about Haman's plan, the king ordered that Haman be killed.

Hannah — She prayed that if God would bless her with a son, she would give the boy back to God. When God gave her a son, as she'd promised, she took Samuel to the priest, Eli, to be raised in the temple. Each year Hannah would weave a coat for her son and take it to him.

Hebrews — These were the Israelites, the descendants of Abraham.

Isaac — He was the son of the elderly couple, Abraham and Sarah. The name Isaac means "laughter." Isaac's parents laughed when God promised them that they would have a son. Isaac married Rebekah and had twin sons, Esau and Jacob.

Isaiah — He was a great prophet of the Old Testament. In a vision, Isaiah saw a seraph touch his lips with a hot coal to signify that he had been cleansed. His sins were forgiven and he could go out and preach the gospel.

Israelites — These people belonged to the nation of Israel, God's chosen people.

Jacob — He was the twin brother of Esau, the son of Isaac and Rebekah. Jacob traded a bowl of stew for Esau's birthright. Jacob also tricked his father into giving him the blessing that belonged to his brother, Esau. Jacob married Rachel and Leah, and altogether he had twelve sons, from whom the twelve tribes of Israel descended.

Japheth — He was one of Noah's three sons. It is believed that Japheth's children were a branch of people who settled north and west of the Fertile Crescent. Japheth and his wife were on the ark with Noah during the Flood.

Jeremiah — This man was called "the weeping prophet" because of his emotional writings. He advised kings, and when he was accused of treason, he was thrown into a cistern.

Jesse — He was the father of eight sons and was an important man in Bethlehem. His youngest son, David, became one of the most famous kings of Israel.

Joash — He was crowned the king of Israel when he was only seven years old. During his reign, he had the Temple repaired from damage that was done by pagan worshipers.

Job — He was a faithful man of God who was tested by Satan. God allowed Satan to take away Job's wealth, family, and health, but Job remained faithful to God.

Jonah — He was one of the minor prophets of the Old Testament. After refusing to go to Nineveh and preach the gospel, he was swallowed by a large fish and sat in the belly of the fish for three days until he decided to obey God.

Joseph — He was the favorite son of his father, Jacob. He was sold into slavery by his brothers and was taken to Egypt. While in Egypt, he was wrongly accused and thrown into prison, where he discovered that he could interpret dreams. He later became second in command of Egypt and saved the country from a terrible famine.

Joshua — He succeeded Moses in leading the Israelites. Joshua led the people in the famous victory over Jericho. When the Israelites reached Canaan, Joshua sent twelve spies into the land, and he eventually led the Israelites into the Promised Land.

Kilion — He was one of Naomi's sons, and was Orpah's husband.

Lot — A nephew of Abraham, Lot and his wife lived in the wicked city of Sodom. Angels warned Lot to take his family and leave the city before God burned it to the ground.

Mahlon — He was one of Naomi's sons, and was Ruth's husband.

Meshach — He was one of the Hebrew men who, because he refused to bow to King Nebuchadnezzar's golden idol, was thrown into a fiery furnace. While Meshach was in the furnace with Shadrach and Abednego, God protected them and they came out unharmed.

Midianites — These were the descendants of Midian, the son of Abraham and Keturah.

Miriam — She was the older sister of Moses and Aaron, and became known as a prophetess. She watched the basket that her brother, Moses, was in as it floated in the Nile River. She was with Moses and the Israelites during their exodus from Egypt and their wandering in the desert.

Moses — He was the man God used to deliver the Israelites from Egyptian slavery. Moses was raised as an Egyptian, but found out later he was a Hebrew. He left Egypt and followed God by leading his people out of Egypt. God spoke to him through a burning bush and also gave him the Ten Commandments on Mount Sinai to give to the Israelites.

Naaman — This Syrian officer was plagued with leprosy. The prophet, Elisha, told him to wash in the Jordan River seven times. When Naaman reluctantly followed Elisha's instructions, he was completely cured of his leprosy.

Naomi — She left her home in Bethlehem during a famine and moved to Moab. While there, her two sons married Ruth and Orpah, two Moabite women. After the death of her husband and sons, Naomi decided to go back to Bethlehem, and Ruth left her own family to go with Naomi.

Nebuchadnezzar (King) — A powerful king of Babylon, he is known for capturing Jerusalem and destroying the Temple. He was the king that threw Shadrach, Meshach, and Abednego into the fiery furnace for refusing to bow down to a golden idol.

Nehemiah — He gathered together many of the Jews who were in exile in Babylon and took them back to Jerusalem to rebuild the wall that had been destroyed many years earlier.

Noah — He was a righteous man chosen by God to build an ark to protect his family and two of every living creature from the flood. Noah's sons, Shem, Ham, and Japheth, are said to be the ancestors of the ancient Middle Eastern tribes.

Oholiab — This skilled craftsman was appointed by Moses to help build the Tabernacle.

Orpah — This Moabite woman married Kilion, one of Naomi's sons. After Orpah's husband died, she went back to live with her mother.

Philistines — These were warlike people who occupied the territory known as Philistia. They were the principle enemy of ancient Israel between 1200 B.C. and 1000 B.C.

priests — These were authorized ministers, advisors of the king. Members of the tribe of Levi in the Old Testament, they represented the people before God through the system of sacrifices.

high priest — This man would represent the nation of Israel before Jehovah. The head of the priests and the spiritual leader of Israel, he was the only one allowed to enter the Holy of Holies, which he did once a year on the Day of Atonement to atone for his own sins and the sins of the people.

Prophets of Baal — These men served and worshiped the god, Baal. It was these prophets who were defeated by Elijah.

Rebekah — She was the wife of Isaac and was the great-niece of Abraham. After being childless for many years, she was blessed with twin sons, Esau and Jacob. She favored Jacob and helped him to trick his father, Isaac, into giving Jacob a blessing.

Ruth — She was the daughter-in-law of Naomi, and the wife of Mahlon. After the death of her husband, Ruth went to Bethlehem with Naomi. There, she met and married a man named Boaz. King David and Jesus were descendants of Ruth and Boaz.

Samson — He was a Nazirite with the gift of strength. He killed thirty Philistines at one time and killed a lion bare-handed. When Delilah tricked him into telling the secret of his strength, the Philistines tied him up, gouged out his eyes, and humiliated him. God gave him his strength one last time. When Samson pushed apart the columns of the Philistine temple, all of the people inside the temple were killed.

Samuel — He was the last of the judges and the first of the prophets. His mother, Hannah, took him to the temple at a young age to train with Eli, the priest, in the ways of God. Samuel had the privilege of anointing both Saul and David as kings of Israel.

Sarah — She was the half-sister of Abraham, and became his wife. After being barren for many years, she gave birth to a son, Isaac, in her old age.

Saul — He was crowned the first king of Israel. He was known for standing a head taller than any other man. He was energetic and courageous. During his reign, he went through depressing times and eventually committed suicide. He was also disobedient to God, which contributed to his downfall.

seraphs — These heavenly beings, similar to angels, stood before God when He appeared to Isaiah. Isaiah said that these beings had six wings: two to cover their faces, two to cover their feet, and two with which to fly.

Shem — The oldest son of Noah, Shem is the ancestor of the Semitic peoples, including the Hebrews. Shem and his wife were on the ark with his father, Noah, during the Flood.

Shadrach — He was one of the three Hebrew men who were thrown into a fiery furnace by King Nebuchadnezzar because they wouldn't bow down to the king's golden idol.

Solomon — He was the son of David and Bathsheba and followed David as king of Israel. While he was king, he had the Temple built. He was known for his great wisdom.

Uzzah — He helped King David by carrying the ark of the covenant back to Jerusalem. When the ark was about to fall, he reached out to grab it. God had specifically said that no one was to touch the ark, so when Uzzah did, he died instantly.

Xerxes (King) — He was the king of Persia who chose the young Jewish girl, Esther, to be his queen. When Xerxes found out that his prime minister, Haman, was plotting to kill the Jews, he ordered that Haman was to be killed.

BibleStoryCards™

1. Card Scramble
Mix up all of the Bible Story Cards. When you give the signal, have the children put the cards in the correct sequential order. You can have the children do this individually or in groups of two or three.

2. Give Me a Clue
Have the children sit in a circle. Then, have one child hold one of the Bible Story Cards on his forehead (make sure he doesn't look at the card). Let the other children give one- or two-word clues to see if the child can guess the story or the Bible person.

3. Overhead Game
Divide the children into two teams. Have one child from each team come forward and face the other children, with his back to the overhead. Write the name of a Bible person on the overhead. Have the children from one team give their teammate a total of three one-word clues. If he can guess who the Bible character is, then his team gets a point. If he cannot guess correctly, then the other player gets to guess. If that player cannot guess correctly either, no point is awarded and two new players should come forward.

4. Bible Tic-Tac-Toe
Put a tic-tac-toe board on an overhead projector. Divide your group into two teams. Ask a person on one team a question — you may use the "Who? What? Where? or Why? Review Questions" (see pages 81-90). If he gets it right, his team can put an *X* or an *O* on the board. If he guesses incorrectly, the team loses a turn. Ask questions of each team, alternately. The team with the most points at the end of the game wins.

5. Bible Bingo
Make several copies of a bingo card. Have the children fill in the blank squares with several different Bible people you have discussed. You can use the "Who? Review Questions" (see pages 81-84) to read to the children as clues for marking off the names on their cards. The first person to mark five in a row correctly wins. You may want to use M&M's or Smarties as markers. If so, make sure you have enough so the children can have a few to snack on while they play.

6. Bible Basketball
You will need a Nerf basketball hoop and ball for this game. Hang the basketball hoop on the top of a door. Then make a "foul line" with masking tape about five feet away from the hoop. Divide the children into two teams. Have a child from one team stand at the foul line. Ask the child a review question. If he answers correctly, his team automatically gets five points. The teacher then gives the child the Nerf ball. If the child makes the basket, the team gets an extra five points. If the child answers the question incorrectly, he sits down and a child from the other team goes to the foul line. The first team to get 50 points wins.

7. Name Scramble
This game can be played individually or as teams. Scramble the letters of a Bible character's name and give a clue as to who the person is. (You could use the "Who? Review Questions" on pages 81-84 for ideas.) You could have a list of 10 to 50 names and clues on a sheet of paper. The first person or team to unscramble the names correctly wins. Here are some examples:
   a. I struck a rock with my staff, and water came out of the rock. SMEOS (Moses)
   b. I am a queen and I saved my people from being killed. SHRETE (Esther)
   c. My brothers were jealous of me because my father gave me a beautiful coat. EHOPSJ (Joseph)

8. Character Quotes
You may want to play this game in pairs. Give the children the name of a Bible person (or maybe two or three names). Have each child write down a statement or quote which that Bible person may have said. After you have collected all of the quotes, read them off one at a time. The person, or pair, who can guess the most Bible quotes correctly wins. Obviously, the children can't guess on their own quote. Here are some examples of quotes:
   a. I was a little nervous while I was in the den with the lions. (Daniel)
   b. Why did I take that gold, silver, and coat from Jericho? (Achan)
   c. Wow! I can't believe it! My leprosy is completely gone. (Naaman)
   d. Did you want to talk to me, Eli? I heard you call my name. (Samuel)
   e. Move donkey! Why are you being so stubborn? (Balaam)

9. Bible Pictionary
This game is similar to the television game show "Win, Lose, or Draw". Have several large sheets of white paper (2' x 2' or 3' sheets) and a black marker. Divide children into teams of three or four. If you have a very large group, you may want to have two different games going on at the same time. One team has a person go up to the paper. The leader shows the person the name of a Bible person or a Bible story. Then the person has one or two minutes (whatever you decide) to draw a picture of that person or situation, without saying a word. His teammates try to guess, out loud, the name of the Bible character or situation. If they guess it correctly within your time limit, they get a point. If the drawing team doesn't guess correctly within the time limit, the other team gets to guess. If they guess correctly, they get the point. This is a fun game for girls to play against the boys.

10. What Am I?
This game is similar to "Guess My Name." Write down the names of several Bible nouns on different pieces of paper; for example, "altar," "manna," "ark," "staff," "Tabernacle." Have one child choose a piece of paper. The rest of the group has to ask the child yes or no questions to try and figure out what the noun is. If the noun is "staff," these might be some of the questions:
   a. Do you eat it? No
   b. Do people use them today? No
   c. Is it something you carry? Yes
   d. Is it something that is worn? No
   e. Is it a staff? Yes

11. Guess My Name

Have one person leave the room. The rest of the group will decide on a particular Bible character. Have the person come back into the room. He then must ask the group about this Bible character. His questions need to be specific, because the group can only answer with a yes or no. For example, some questions to ask might be "Is this person a man? Was this person a judge? Was he a shepherd? Was he a king?"

12. Bible Baseball

Have four chairs set up in a diamond shape. Divide your group into two teams. You need to have four different levels of questions. First-base questions "singles" are the easiest. Second-base questions "doubles" are a little harder than singles. Third-base questions "triples" are a little harder than doubles. Home-run questions are the hardest. A player "goes to bat" by sitting in the chair at home plate. You are the "pitcher," and the child asks you for the type of question he would like to answer: single, double, triple, or home run. If he gets the answer to the question right, he gets to go to the appropriate base. If he gets it wrong, he is "out." There are no strikes in this game. When a team gets three outs, the other team goes up to bat. You could make the game a little more interesting by having a "catcher" sit beside the batter. If the catcher (from the other team, of course) answered the question before the batter, the batter would be out. You could have one catcher for the inning, or you could change catchers with each new batter. (To vary the game, you could use the " Story Card Spinner" (see page 110, #19) to determine which kind of question the batter would receive.)

13. Balloon Pop Review

Before you blow up your balloons, put a slip of paper with a review question in each balloon. After you tell the story, divide the group into teams. Have a person from one team pop his balloon. If he can answer the question on his slip of paper, his team gets a point. The team with the most points wins.

14. Bible Charades

This game can be played individually or as teams. Have the children choose one story from the Bible Story Cards. You could have all of the Bible Story Cards in a hat and have the person or group pick a card at random. The individual or group then must act out the story so the other children can try to guess the story or Bible character(s).

15. Beach Ball Review

Blow up a large beach ball. Write review questions on small slips of paper. Fold the slips of paper and put a number on each piece. Then tape the slips of paper to the ball. You will say, "Are you on the ball?" and throw the ball to a child. The child will take slip #1 (and so on) and read the question. If he can answer the question, he will keep the paper and throw the ball back to the teacher. If he cannot answer the question, the slip of paper will need to be taped back onto the ball. Then repeat the question, "Are you on the ball?" and throw the ball to another child. The challenge is for the children to remove all of the slips of paper from the ball in the least amount of time.

16. Who Am I?

Pin the name of a Bible person on the back of each child, making sure they don't see the names on their own backs. When everyone has a "new" name, he must go around and ask the other children questions about himself as if he were the person named on his back. The one rule is that he must ask yes-or-no questions; for example, "Am I a fisherman? Was I a king of Israel? Did I have many brothers?" The first person to come up and tell you who he is, wins.

17. Newspaper Search

Bring several newspapers and pairs of scissors to class. On a blackboard, a bulletin board, or 3-by-5-inch cards, write the names of the Bible characters in your story, the memory verse, specific places in your story, or anything you want to list that has to do with your story. Have the children find the words or the letters to make the words in the newspaper, and then cut them out and piece them together. This would be a fun individual or pair project.

18. Shaving Cream Review

After you have told the Bible story for the day, put a pile of shaving cream in front of each child. Let the children spread out the shaving cream in front of them. (Have a big roll of paper towels handy to wipe the children's hands.) With their fingers, have them draw each part of the Bible story. This will let you know just how much they learned about the story. The shaving cream wipes up easily and *will not* harm clothing. The kids will love it!

19. Story Card Spinner

Make a spinner that has four different sections. (You could use the spinner from a Twister game.) Make separate sections for the "Who? What? Where? and Why? Review Questions" (see pages 81-90). Divide the children into two teams. Have one child from one team spin the pointer on the spinner. Whatever section the pointer lands on determines the question he will receive. If he answers the question correctly, him team gets five points. Whichever team gets to 50 points first is the winner.

20. Card Collection

Divide the children into two teams. Put a set of Bible Story Cards into a bag or hat. Have a child from one team draw a card and give it to you. Then ask the child one of the review questions on the card. If the child can answer the question correctly, his team gets a point and the card goes back into the container. If the child answers incorrectly, hang on to the card. Call a child from the other team and follow the same directions. The object is for one (or both) of the teams to end up with a greater number of points than the number of cards you get.

21. Bible Time Capsule

This game can be played as a group, or you can divide the children into teams. Put all 50 Old Testament Bible Story Cards into a "time capsule." Decorate the time capsule with brightly colored contact or construction paper. Have a child pull a card out of the time capsule without the other children or his team members seeing which one it is. The child has to tell the group or his team members about one thing that the character (or one of the characters) from the story did or accomplished. The object is to see if the group or groups can guess the character. You could vary this game by having the person who draws a card act out a scene from that story for the group or team to guess.

22. Story Diorama

A diorama is a miniature three-dimensional scene made inside a box. These can be made easily inside shoe boxes. The materials needed are shoe boxes, pipe cleaners (to make people), paints, paint brushes, construction paper, cardboard (for buildings), modeling clay, markers and crayons. Have the children work individually or in groups to make dioramas depicting scenes from the stories on the Bible Story Cards. These will be fun to display.

23. Story Review Cards

Find the "Who? What? Where? and Why? Review Questions" and answers on pages 81-90. On 3-by-5-inch cards, put the review questions on the front and the answers on the back. These can be very handy if you have some extra time before a story and want to review previous stories, or the cards can be used as a review after you have told a story. If you have some very eager children, you could put these cards in a learning center where a child could go and review the cards by himself. He could challenge himself by using a timer to see how many questions he could answer correctly within a certain amount of time.

24. Bible Story Map

This idea can be used for several different stories, but is especially interesting when discussing the exodus from Egypt. This project is suited for children in grades 4 through 8. For this project, you will need a Bible atlas or encyclopedia, paper, pencils and/or markers. On a chalkboard or overhead projector, list different places and landmarks from the story that you want to be included on the children's map. Then give each child or pair of children a sheet of paper. Have the children label the places and landmarks you have listed and then mark the route that was traveled. There are blank maps and charts on pages 121-137.

25. Story Card Match

You will want to save this review until you have covered most of the stories. This could be an individual or pairs competition. On a large sheet of paper or a piece of posterboard (you may need several), make enough large squares to list these books of the Old Testament: Genesis, Exodus, Numbers, Joshua, Judges, Ruth, 1 Samuel, 2 Samuel, 1 Kings, 2 Kings, Nehemiah, Esther, Job, Isaiah, Jeremiah, Daniel, and Jonah. Lay the paper or posterboard on a table. Give the set of Old Testament Bible Story Cards to a child or pair of children. When you give the signal, have the child or pair, without looking at the backs of the cards, put each card in the square naming the book where the story is found. Record the number he or they have correct, and give the set of cards to the next child or pair. The child or pair with the most correct is the winner.

26. Bible Story Mural

This would be a very good ongoing project for your children. This project is appropriate for children in grades 3 through 8. You will need to have on hand some Bibles, crayons or markers, pencils, paper, magazines that can be cut up, and glue. After every five or ten stories (your choice) assign each child or pair of children one of the Bible stories. Give each child or group a piece of paper (all the same size). Have the children draw or cut out pictures from the magazines pictures that would represent their stories. When they have finished, label the pictures and hang them on the wall in chronological order. Add to the mural after teaching five or ten more stories (whatever number you have chosen). You will need to determine the size of paper you use by the size of your room — the mural will take up quite a bit of space. You may even want to invite others in to see your project.

27. Bible Story Bag

This game can be played individually or in teams of no more than three. Put the Bible Story Cards in some type of bag. Have each child or team get a card from the bag, without looking at the back of the card. When you say go, the individuals or teams are to turn their cards over and answer the first five review questions on the back. The first person or team to answer all of the questions should let you know by raising hands, or holding up papers or pencils. The first person or team finished that has answered all of the questions correctly wins. You could vary this game by having the students sit in a circle. As you play music, have the children pass the bag with the Bible Story Cards around the circle. When the music stops, the child holding the bag pulls out one card. Have the child answer the question you choose from the first five review questions on that card. If he answers correctly, without looking at the story, he gets to hang onto the card. The child with the most cards at the end of the game wins.

28. Change the Bible Story

Give one Bible Story Card to a child or two children. He or they need to pick three or four sentences (however many you decide) and change them so they are incorrect. Then the entire story should be rewritten on another sheet of paper with the incorrect sentences. Have the children or group trade stories when they are finished. They are to take the stories they have been given and underline the sentences that are incorrect. If you are working with preschool children, you can vary this idea by reading the story aloud to the children, but changing three or four sentences so that they are incorrect. Have the children or groups yell out the correct answer if they think that a sentence is incorrect. For example; if you are reading the story of Jonah, you could say, "Jonah was swallowed by a dinosaur."

29. Tabernacle Model

This project is suggested for children in grades 5 through 8. The children can work in pairs or groups of two or three for this project. You will need to do a little research in a Bible encyclopedia or dictionary. It would be helpful to have these resources available for your children too. The following materials are suggested for this project: several pieces of cardboard, modeling clay, construction paper, crayons, markers, glue, tape, stapler, staples, and cloth. Have the children work in small groups to build models of the Tabernacle using these materials, and have them create and label specific parts of the Tabernacle (i.e. court, altar, Holy Place, Most Holy Place, ark of the covenant, etc.). A picture of the Tabernacle is listed on page 130 of this guide.

30. Temple Model

This project is suggested for children in grades 4 through 8. You can read the description of Solomon's Temple in 2 Chronicles 3 and 4. Have the children work in small groups to build sugar-cube models of the Temple on the cardboard pieces. Time permitting, have the children paint their temple when it is completed. The materials you will need are a Bible encyclopedia, sugar cubes, glue, 9-by-12-inch pieces of cardboard and possibly tempra paint and brushes. The measurements of the Temple were 90 feet long by 30 feet wide by 45 feet high. It would be easy to use a scale of 1 inch to 10 feet. Pictures of the Temple are shown on pages 136-137 of this guide.

BibleStoryCards™

1. Memory Verse Book
During each session, have every child write the memory verse for that week in some type of notebook or booklet. Have them take their booklets home and memorize the verse before the next lesson. If a child has memorized the verse by the next session, put a star at the top of the page where the verse is written. Each time the child is able to recite the verse from the previous lesson, give him another star.

2. Memory Verse Mix
Cut out several square pieces of felt. Write each word of a memory verse on a separate piece of felt. Be sure to write the reference on one piece. Mix up the squares on a flannelboard. Have the children take turns putting the words in the correct order and then say the verse out loud.

3. Memory Verse Envelope
This game is similar to "Memory Verse Mix." Put each word of a memory verse on a separate piece of paper. Mix the pieces of paper and put them into an envelope. Make up enough envelopes to give one to each child or pair of children. All the envelopes could contain the same verse or different verses. The first child or pair to put the memory verse together correctly is the winner.

4. Memory Verse Card Drill
On one piece of 8-by-11-inch sheet of cardboard or construction paper, write the first half of a memory verse. Do this with several different verses. Hold up one of these cards. The first child to finish the memory verse (and give the verse reference) gets to keep the card. The child with the most cards at the end of the game is the winner. A variation for older children would be to put memory verse references on the cards, and a child must say an entire verse correctly to get a card.

5. Clothespin Review
Have each word of a memory verse written on a 3-by-5-inch card or piece of paper. String a rope across the room and attach the cards to the rope with clothespins. Put up the cards in an incorrect order, and then have the children take turns putting the cards in the right order on the rope.

6. Memory Verse Pocket
Cut a piece of cardboard into two- or three-inch strips. Then cut the strips into rectangles. Write each word of a memory verse on the end of one of the rectangles. Next, secure several different "pockets" onto a board of some kind. They will need to be placed in rows. Make sure the pockets are large enough for the cardboard pieces to slide easily into them. Give each child one of the rectangle cards. The object is for the children to put the words of the verse in the correct order. Have each child, one at a time, put his card into the pocket where he thinks it belongs. If the cards do not end up in the correct order, take them out and repeat the process until the children put the words in the pockets correctly. When the verse is correct, have the children say it together.

7. Memory Verse Match

On a card or a piece of paper write a memory verse and reference. Make several of these, using the same verse or different verses on each card. Then, cut the cards into two pieces, so that the reference and half of the verse are on one side of the card, and the rest of the verse is on the other side of the card. Put the cards into a pile and have each child draw one piece of a card. When you give the signal, have the children try to find their "match." For older children, you could make this a little more difficult. When you are writing the verses on the cards, change a word or part of the reference of each verse to make it incorrect. Then, after the children find their partners, have them tell you what mistakes were on their cards. Have Bibles handy — the children may need to look up their memory verses.

8. Clue Word Memory Cards

Think of three to five words to serve as clues for a memory verse. Write each clue word on a separate card. Number the cards, with #1 indicating the most difficult clue, and the highest number indicating the least difficult. Divide the children into two teams. Show one team the most difficult clue (cover up the others). If no one from that team can recite the verse, show the clue to the other team. If the other team cannot recite the verse on the first clue, go back to the first team and give them the second clue. Keep doing this until the memory verse is correctly recited, and give the card to the team that recited the verse. The team with the most cards at the end of the game wins. A variation would be to give a point value to each clue. For instance, if a team gets the verse right on the first clue, they get 10 points; second clue, 8 points; third clue, 6 points; fourth clue, 4 points; and fifth clue, 2 points. The first team to get 50 points would be the winner.

9. Pass the Hat

For each memory verse, have two 3-by-5-inch cards available. On one card, write the entire memory verse, and on the other card write the verse reference. Do this with several verses. Put all of the cards into a hat, and have the children sit in a circle. As you play music, have the children pass the hat around the circle. When you stop the music, the child holding the hat needs to pull out one of the cards. If he pulls out a memory verse, he needs to recite the verse reference. If he pulls out a verse reference, he needs to recite the memory verse. A variation of this would be to divide the children into pairs and have all of the cards in a pile. Then, have one pair of children match each memory verse with its reference. Time each of the pairs as they do this. The pair with the fastest time is the winner.

10. Chalkboard Verse

Print the memory verse on the chalkboard. Have the children, or each child individually, recite the verse. Then erase a letter or word. Have the children recite the verse again as though the missing letters or words were still there. Continue to do this until all of the words are gone, having each child or the group continue to say the verse.

11. Memory Balloon-a-Thon

You will need three different colors of balloons (e.g., red, green, and blue) and three boxes. This review game can be used for many different purposes. This game is good for reviewing memory verses, but you can also use it to review specific scenes of a Bible story. For each set of same-color balloons, put each word of a memory verse or description of a scene from a story on a slip of paper, put the paper in separate balloons and blow up the balloons. Put all of the same-color balloons in a box. Divide the children into three teams and have them line up at a starting line. When you say go, have the first person in line take a balloon from his team's box, sit on the balloon until it pops, and bring back the slip of paper. He is to tag the next person in line, who will do the same thing. When everyone on the team has brought back his slip of paper, the team is to put their memory verse together and say it as a group (or act out the scene from the story). The first group to finish is the winner.

12. Catch a Verse

On a 3-by-5-inch card, write one memory verse reference. It would be fun to cut the cards in the shape of fish. On each card (or fish), place a paper clip. Put the "fish" into some type of bowl. Next, make a "fishing" pole from a yardstick or dowel stick, and put a magnet on the end of the string. Give each child a chance to go "fishing." When the child pulls out a memory verse reference, if he can say the verse correctly, he gets to keep the fish. If he doesn't say the verse correctly, he has to throw the fish back into the "water." The child who collects the most fish by the end of the game is the winner.

13. Guess a Letter

This game is very similar to "Wheel of Fortune." Draw a square or a blank line for each letter in a memory verse. Have a child guess a letter. If that letter is in the verse, write it in the appropriate blank(s). Let the child keep guessing letters until he guesses incorrectly. You could simplify this game by letting the children guess individual words. When they guess correctly, go ahead and fill in the entire word wherever it appears in the verse. You have the option of writing the verse reference on the board above the blanks for the verse or making the reference part of the puzzle. The first person to say the entire verse correctly wins.

14. Round Table Memory

Have the children sit in a circle. Have the memory verse on a board where it can be easily seen. As you go around the circle, give each child one word of the memory verse to remember. Then, start at the beginning of the verse, and slowly have each child say his word in the correct order to complete the verse. Gradually, you can have the children say the verse faster. At some point, take away the board with the memory verse and have the children continue to say the verse. A variation of this would be to have the first child in the circle say the first word of the verse. Then, the next child would say the first word and the second word, and so on until the last person says the entire memory verse.

15. Memory Choir

Divide your group into these four different sections of a choir: (1) sopranos, (2) altos, (3) tenors, and (4) basses. If you have a large group, you may want to divide them into two separate groups before you assign them their parts. As you "direct" the choir, indicate with raised fingers (according to the above list) which part of the choir you want to say or sing the memory verse. A variation of this game would be to divide the group into soloists, duets, trios, and quartets.

16. Memory Ladder

Give each child a large sheet of paper. Have the children draw the side bars of a ladder. Cut out several paper "rungs" for their ladders ahead of time. Each time a child memorizes a memory verse, have him write the reference on a rung and then glue it onto his paper to form a ladder. See who can get to the top of the ladder first.

17. Memory Verse Square

With a marker, divide a piece of posterboard into twelve different squares. In each square, write a number (1 – 12) and a memory verse reference. Have a child roll two dice. Whatever number they roll, they need to look for that number on the board. Then, they need to read the verse reference and correctly say the entire memory verse. See who can say the most memory verses without making a mistake. If your children are very competitive, you may want to think of some type of scoring system for this review.

18. Memory Verse Golf

To make the golf course, take an egg carton and cut off the lid and side flap. You will need two straws, with each cut into three pieces. Out of construction paper, cut out six small triangles. Number the triangles and glue them onto the straws to make flags. Then place the straws into the center peaks of the egg carton. Divide the children into two teams. One team will "golf" from one "hole" to the next along one side of the carton, and the other team along the other side. Use two golf balls as markers or draw or make two different "golfers" to be the markers. Take turns asking members of the teams questions about a memory verse or giving them a verse reference and having them recite the verse for you. If a child answers correctly, his team gets a "hole in one" and gets to move to the next hole. If he answers incorrectly, the marker is moved back to hole #1. The first team to get to hole #6 is the winner.

19. Memory Verse Puppet

This activity would be very good for preschool children. You could use a manufactured puppet, or even one that you have made, to recite the memory verse to the children. It would be easy to make a puppet out of a regular lunch-size paper sack. Just draw a happy face on the puppet, use yarn to give it some hair, and you have an instant puppet. Have the puppet explain what the memory verse means and how it relates to the Bible story. After repeating the verse several times, you may want to have the children take turns using the puppet to say the verse.

20. Memory Verse Sticks

On white drinking straws, write several different memory verse references, one per straw. Hold these "sticks" (straws) upright on the floor or a table, and let go of them. Have one child try to pick up one of the sticks without moving any of the other sticks. Once a child touches a stick, he can try to pick up only that stick. He cannot let go of that stick and try to pick up another one. If the child successfully picks up a stick without moving any other stick, he then must read the memory verse reference and recite that verse. If he recites the verse correctly, he gets to keep the stick. The person with the most sticks at the end of the game wins.

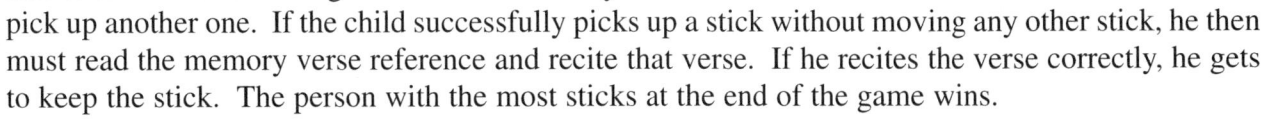

21. Balloon Pop Race

Divide the children into two teams. Have the children on each team number off. This works best with an even number of children on each team (or one child can take two turns). Have the teams stand on either side of the room and have a pile of non-inflated balloons in the center of the room. To start the game, you need to call out a memory verse reference. Tell the children to listen carefully because you can only say it one time. After you say the reference, call out a number. The child from each team who has been given that number is to go to the center of the room, pick up a balloon, blow it up, pop it, then say the entire memory verse. The first person to do this wins a point for his team. The team with the most points at the end of the game wins.

22. Memory Verse Mobile

Create mobiles out of clothes hangers, dowels, and string. With construction paper, have the children cut out different shapes. On the shapes, have the children write words or groups of words from a memory verse. For example, for Genesis 1:1 a child might cut out the shape of a big number "1" and write "In the beginning" on it. He might then cut out a triangle and write "God created" on it, then a cloud with "the heavens" and a circle (representing the earth) with "and the earth." On another shape he could write the memory reference.

23. Name That Verse

This game is very similar to the old television game show "Name That Tune." Divide the children into two different groups and have one person from each group come to the front. Instruct the children that you will be giving them a clue to the memory verse. You may give the book or the entire reference where the verse is found, the name of the person who originally said the verse, or some other clue. Then, have one child start by telling you, "I can say that verse in ——— words" (the number will vary, depending on the number of words the child thinks it will take for him to guess the verse). The child's opponent will counter by saying, "I can say that verse in ———words" (a smaller number than the first child said). If the first child says, "Name that verse!" the teacher will say the number of words from the verse requested by the opponent, who then must finish the verse and the reference correctly. If the verse is quoted correctly, that team receives a point. The team with the most points at the end of the game wins.

24. Memory Verse Bulletin Board

You will need three different colors of 3-by-5-inch cards (e.g., pink, yellow, and green) and some Velcro strips. Choose several different memory verses. Using one set of same-color cards, write the first half of each memory verse on a separate card. Using another set of same-color cards, write the rest of each verse on a separate card. Write each verse reference on a card from the third set. To make the cards last longer, you may want to have them laminated. On the back of each card, put a small strip of Velcro. On your bulletin board, put three long strips of Velcro so that the cards will stick to the board. On the first row, mix up the first group of cards. On the second row, mix up the second group of cards. And on the third row, mix up the cards with the references. Have a child go up to the board and try to put the cards in the correct order, lining up the memory verses and references from top to bottom. This could be used as an independent activity for children who finish other projects ahead of time.

BibleStoryCards™

1. Bible Biography
Hold up one of the memory objects. Have one child tell which story goes with that memory object. If he is correct, then hold up the Bible Story Card to go with that object and have the child tell everything he knows about that story, or have him answer the review questions on the back of the card. For older children who want to do a little research, have them choose one of the Bible people they have learned about. Then have the children use a Bible and a concordance to look up further information about that person. Have them draw five or ten different pictures on the life of that person.

2. Object Match
Have at least five to ten different Bible Story Cards on a table with the memory objects that go with the stories. Mix up the cards and the objects. Have each child or pair of children match each object with its story. Try to see who can match the objects with the story cards in the fastest time.

3. Object Bag
Have several different memory objects in a large bag. Have a child pull out one object and tell about the Bible story which goes with that object. For older children, you could make this more challenging by having them not only tell about the story, but also say the memory verse that goes with the story.

4. Name That Object
Divide your children into teams. Put all of the Bible Story Cards that you have in a covered box or a bag. Pull out one of the cards. Have a child from one team tell you what memory object goes with that story and why the object is associated with the story. If the child is correct, he gets a point for his team. The team with the most points at the end of the game wins.

5. Object Sequence
Lay out all of the objects you have used up to this point. Have an individual child or a group of children try to put the objects in the correct order according to the sequence of their corresponding stories.

6. Musical Objects
Have the children sit in a circle on the floor. Pick three or four memory objects to pass around the circle. Play some music and have the children slowly pass the objects around the circle. When the music stops, whoever is holding an object must do one of the following:
   a. Say the memory verse for that story.
   b. Tell one important fact about the story the object represents.

7. Object Poster

Give each child a different Bible Story Card and a blank 8 -by-11 inch sheet of paper. Have the child draw a picture on the paper of the memory object that goes with his story card. You could have magazines available and have each child cut out a picture of the object to paste onto the paper. When everyone is finished, have each child hold up his picture and tell about the Bible story that goes with the object. Or, you could have each child hold up his picture and have one of the other children try to name the object and the story it represents.

8. Object Mural

Have a long sheet of paper, and use a marker to draw lines dividing the paper evenly into ten to twelve different squares. Put a number in the corner of each square, corresponding with the number of one of the Bible Story Cards you have worked with at some point. Give each child a number, and then have him look at the card that corresponds with that number. In his square, have him draw the memory object that goes with his story. After all of the children have drawn their pictures, hang the mural on the wall and have each child tell about the story that goes with the object he drew. To vary this, each child could pick any object on the mural and tell about that story, or you could talk about the objects and their stories with the children as a group.

9. Memory Object Bookmark

Have construction paper, scissors, crayons, markers, glue, and appropriate stickers available. For younger children, cut 2-by-6-inch strips of colored construction paper to use as bookmarks. Older children can cut out the strips for themselves. On their bookmarks, have the children each draw a picture of the memory object for the story you are studying. Also, have them list the Bible story reference. This activity not only will help the children to associate the memory object with the story, but it also will help them to learn where the Bible story is found.

THE OLD TESTAMENT BOOKSHELF

The word "testament" means "will" or "covenant." The term "Old Testament," therefore, refers first to God's covenant or promise-law to bless mankind through the Jewish nation. It has also come to refer to the *writings about* the Old Covenant, although, strictly speaking, these ancient books are the Old Covenant *Scriptures.*

Purpose/Theme:
The Scriptures of the Old Testament record the story of God's chosen people, Israel, and their relationship to His covenant to bless all nations through them.

The Books of Law
Genesis | Exodus | Leviticus | Numbers | Deuteronomy

The Books of History
Joshua | Judges | Ruth | First Samuel | Second Samuel | First Kings | Second Kings | First Chronicles | Second Chronicles | Ezra | Nehemiah | Esther

The Books of Poetry
Job | Psalms | Proverbs | Ecclesiastes | Song of Songs

The Books of Major Prophets
Isaiah | Jeremiah | Lamentations | Ezekiel | Daniel

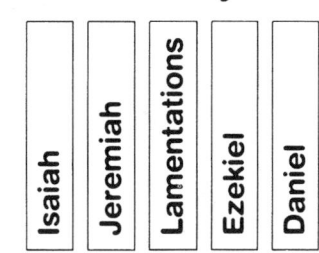

The Books of Minor Prophets
Hosea | Joel | Amos | Obadiah | Jonah | Micah | Nahum | Habakkuk | Zephaniah | Haggai | Zechariah | Malachi

Reprinted from *The Bible Visual Resource Book,* © 1989 by Gospel Light Publications, Regal Books, Ventura, CA 93003. Used by permission.

WHEN OLD TESTAMENT EVENTS HAPPENED

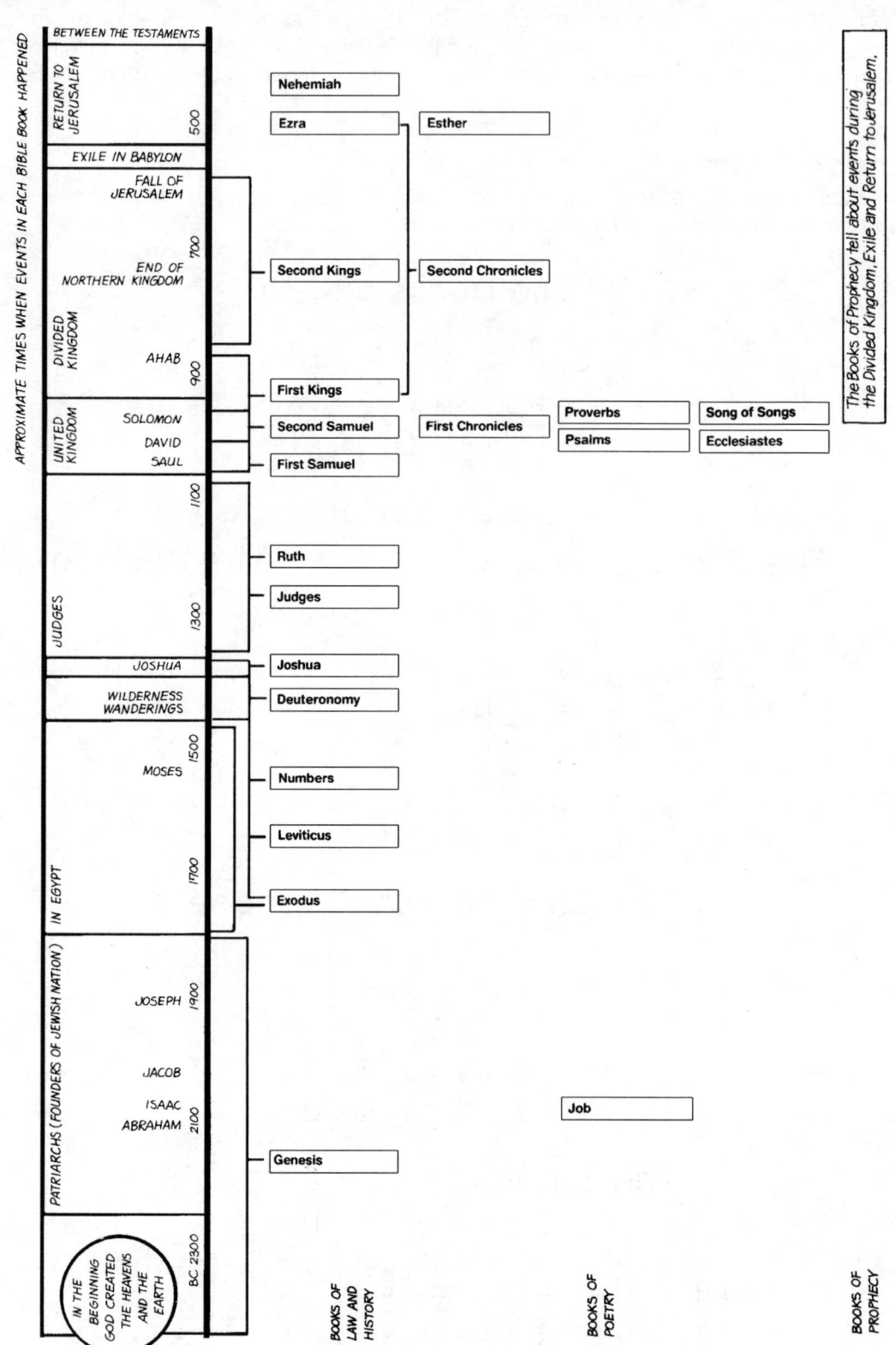

Timeline (APPROXIMATE TIMES WHEN EVENTS IN EACH BIBLE BOOK HAPPENED)

BETWEEN THE TESTAMENTS

- RETURN TO JERUSALEM — 500
  - Nehemiah
  - Ezra
  - Esther

EXILE IN BABYLON
- FALL OF JERUSALEM
- END OF NORTHERN KINGDOM — 700
  - Second Kings
  - Second Chronicles

DIVIDED KINGDOM
- AHAB — 900
  - First Kings

UNITED KINGDOM
- SOLOMON
- DAVID
- SAUL
  - Second Samuel
  - First Chronicles
  - Proverbs
  - Song of Songs
  - Psalms
  - Ecclesiastes
  - First Samuel — 1100

JUDGES
- Ruth
- Judges — 1300

JOSHUA
- Joshua

WILDERNESS WANDERINGS
- Deuteronomy

MOSES — 1500
- Numbers
- Leviticus

IN EGYPT — 1700
- Exodus

PATRIARCHS (FOUNDERS OF JEWISH NATION)
- JOSEPH — 1900
- JACOB
- ISAAC
- ABRAHAM — 2100
  - Genesis
  - Job

BC 2300 — IN THE BEGINNING GOD CREATED THE HEAVENS AND THE EARTH

BOOKS OF LAW AND HISTORY

BOOKS OF POETRY

BOOKS OF PROPHECY

The Books of Prophecy tell about events during the Divided Kingdom, Exile and Return to Jerusalem.

Reprinted from *The Bible Visual Resource Book*, © 1989 by Gospel Light Publications, Regal Books, Ventura, CA 93003. Used by permission.

RULERS OF ISRAEL & JUDAH

DATA AND DATES IN ORDER OF SEQUENCE

#	Reference	Ruler	Synchronism	Length	Notes	Dates
1.	1Ki 12:1-24; 14:21-31	Rehoboam (Judah)		17 years		930-913
2.	1Ki 12:25—14:20	Jeroboam I (Israel)		22 years		930-909
3.	1Ki 15:1-8	Abijah (Judah)	18th of Jeroboam	3 years		913-910
4.	1Ki 15:9-24	Asa (Judah)	20th of Jeroboam	41 years		910-869
5.	1Ki 15:25-31	Nadab (Israel)	2nd of Asa	2 years		909-908
6.	1Ki 15:32—16:7	Baasha (Israel)	3rd of Asa	24 years		908-886
7.	1Ki 16:8-14	Elah (Israel)	26th of Asa	2 years		886-885
8.	1Ki 16:15-20	Zimri (Israel)	27th of Asa	7 days		885
9.	1Ki 16:21-22	Tibni (Israel)			Overlap with Omri	885-880
10.	1Ki 16:23-28	Omri (Israel)	27th of Asa	12 years	Made king by the people	885
					Overlap with Tibni	885-880
					Official reign = 11 actual years	885-874
			31st of Asa		Beginning of sole reign	880
11.	1Ki 16:29—22:40	Ahab (Israel)	38th of Asa	22 years	Official reign = 21 actual years	874-853
12.	1Ki 22:41-50	Jehoshaphat (Judah)		25 years	Co-regency with Asa	872-869
			4th of Ahab		Official reign	872-848
					Beginning of sole reign	869
					Has Jehoram as regent	853-848
13.	1Ki 22:51—2Ki 1:18	Ahaziah (Israel)	17th of Jehoshaphat	2 years	Official reign = 1 yr. actual reign	853-852
14.	2Ki 1:17; 3:1—8:15	Joram (Israel)	2nd of Jehoram; 18th of Jehoshaphat	12 years	Official reign = 11 actual years	852-841
					Beginning of sole reign	848
15.	2Ki 8:16-24	Jehoram (Judah)	5th of Joram	8 years	Official reign = 7 actual years	848-841
16.	2Ki 8:25-29; 2Ki 9:29	Ahaziah (Judah)	12th of Joram; 11th of Joram	1 year	Nonaccession-year reckoning	841
					Accession-year reckoning	841
17.	2Ki 9:30—10:36	Jehu (Israel)		28 years		841-814
18.	2Ki 11	Athaliah (Judah)		7 years		841-835
19.	2Ki 12	Joash (Judah)	7th of Jehu	40 years		835-796
20.	2Ki 13:1-9	Jehoahaz (Israel)	23rd of Joash	17 years		814-798
21.	2Ki 13:10-25	Jehoash (Israel)	37th of Joash	16 years		798-782
22.	2Ki 14:1-22	Amaziah (Judah)	2nd of Jehoash	29 years	Overlap with Azariah	796-767
					Total reign	792-767
23.	2Ki 14:23-29	Jeroboam II (Israel)		41 years	Co-regency with Jehoash	793-782
					Beginning of sole reign	782
24.	2Ki 15:1-7	Azariah (Judah)	15th of Amaziah	52 years	Overlap with Amaziah	792-767
			27th of Jeroboam		Total reign	792-740
					Beginning of sole reign	767
25.	2Ki 15:8-12	Zechariah (Israel)	38th of Azariah	6 months		753
26.	2Ki 15:13-15	Shallum (Israel)	39th of Azariah	1 month		752
27.	2Ki 15:16-22	Menahem (Israel)	39th of Azariah	10 years	Ruled in Samaria	752-742
28.	2Ki 15:23-26	Pekahiah (Israel)	50th of Azariah	2 years		742-740
29.	2Ki 15:27-31	Pekah (Israel)		20 years	In Gilead, overlapping years	752-740
					Total reign	752-732
			52nd of Azariah		Beginning of sole reign	740
30.	2Ki 15:32-38; 2Ki 15:30	Jotham (Judah)		16 years	Co-regency with Azariah	750-740
					Official reign	750-735
					Reign to his 20th year	750-732
			2nd of Pekah		Beginning of co-regency	750
					Total reign	735-715
31.	2Ki 16	Ahaz (Judah)	17th of Pekah	16 years	From 20th of Jotham	735
					20th of Jotham	732-715
32.	2Ki 15:30; 2Ki 17	Hoshea (Israel)	12th of Ahaz*	9 years		732
33.	2Ki 18:1—20:21	Hezekiah (Judah)	3rd of Hoshea*	29 years	Co-regency with Hezekiah	715-686
34.	2Ki 21:1-18	Manasseh (Judah)		55 years	Total reign	697-686
35.	2Ki 21:19-26	Amon (Judah)		2 years		697-642
36.	2Ki 22:1—23:30	Josiah (Judah)		31 years		642-640
37.	2Ki 23:31-33	Jehoahaz (Judah)		3 months		640-609
38.	2Ki 23:34—24:7	Jehoiakim (Judah)		11 years		609
39.	2Ki 24:8-17	Jehoiachin (Judah)		3 months		609-598
40.	2Ki 24:18—25:26	Zedekiah (Judah)		11 years		598-597
						597-586

*These data arise when the reign of Hoshea is thrown 12 years in advance of its historical position.

Italics denote kings of Judah.
Non-italic type denotes kings of **Israel**.

Adapted from *A Chronology of the Hebrew Kings* by Edwin R. Thiele © 1977 by The Zondervan Corporation. Used by permission.

Reprinted from *The Bible Visual Resource Book,* © 1989 by Gospel Light Publications, Regal Books, Ventura, CA 93003. Used by permission.

TIMES OF THE PROPHETS

Books of Major Prophets: Isaiah, Jeremiah, Lamentations, Ezekiel, Daniel

The Books of Minor Prophets: Hosea, Joel, Amos, Obadiah, Jonah, Micah, Nahum, Habakkuk, Zephaniah, Haggai, Zechariah, Malachi

Israel's prophets are a built-in "reformation" aspect of Old Testament faith. The word "prophet" means "to speak out"—to *forth-tell* God's word as much as to foretell the future. They spoke out against hypocrisy, injustice, immorality and idolatry, warning God's people that He would punish them for such continued disobedience. The prophets also foretold the time when God would save a remnant of His people through whom all nations would be blessed.

Timeline 1 (1040 BC – 790 BC)

Prophet: Samuel

Kings of united monarchy: Saul, David, Solomon

Northern Kingdom Israel (930 – 790): Jeroboam, Baasha, Omri, Ahab, Jehoram, Jehu, Jehoahaz, Jehoash
Dates: 930, 910, 885, 875, 850, 840, 815, 800, 790

Prophets: Elijah, Elisha, Joel

Southern Kingdom Judah (930 – 790): Rehoboam, Asa, Jehoshaphat, Jehoram, Joash, Amaziah
Dates: 930, 910, 870, 853, 835, 795, 790

Note: Some minor kings are omitted from this chart.

Timeline 2 (790 – 415 BC)

Northern Kingdom (Israel) (790 – 720): Jeroboam II, Menahem, Pekah, Hoshea — **Fall of Northern Kingdom (Israel)**
Dates: 790, 750, 740, 730, 720

Prophets: Jonah, Amos, Micah, Isaiah, Hosea, Jeremiah, Zephaniah, Habakkuk, Nahum, Daniel, Ezekiel, Obadiah, Zechariah, Haggai, Malachi

Southern Kingdom Judah / Post-exile: Uzziah, Jotham, Ahaz, Hezekiah, Manasseh, Josiah, Jehoiakim, Zedekiah — **Jerusalem and Temple Destroyed** — Zerubbabel, Ezra, Nehemiah
Dates: 790, 750, 735, 715, 695, 640, 610, 600, 585, 540, 460, 445, 415

Reprinted from *The Bible Visual Resource Book*, © 1989 by Gospel Light Publications, Regal Books, Ventura, CA 93003. Used by permission.

LAND OF ABRAHAM

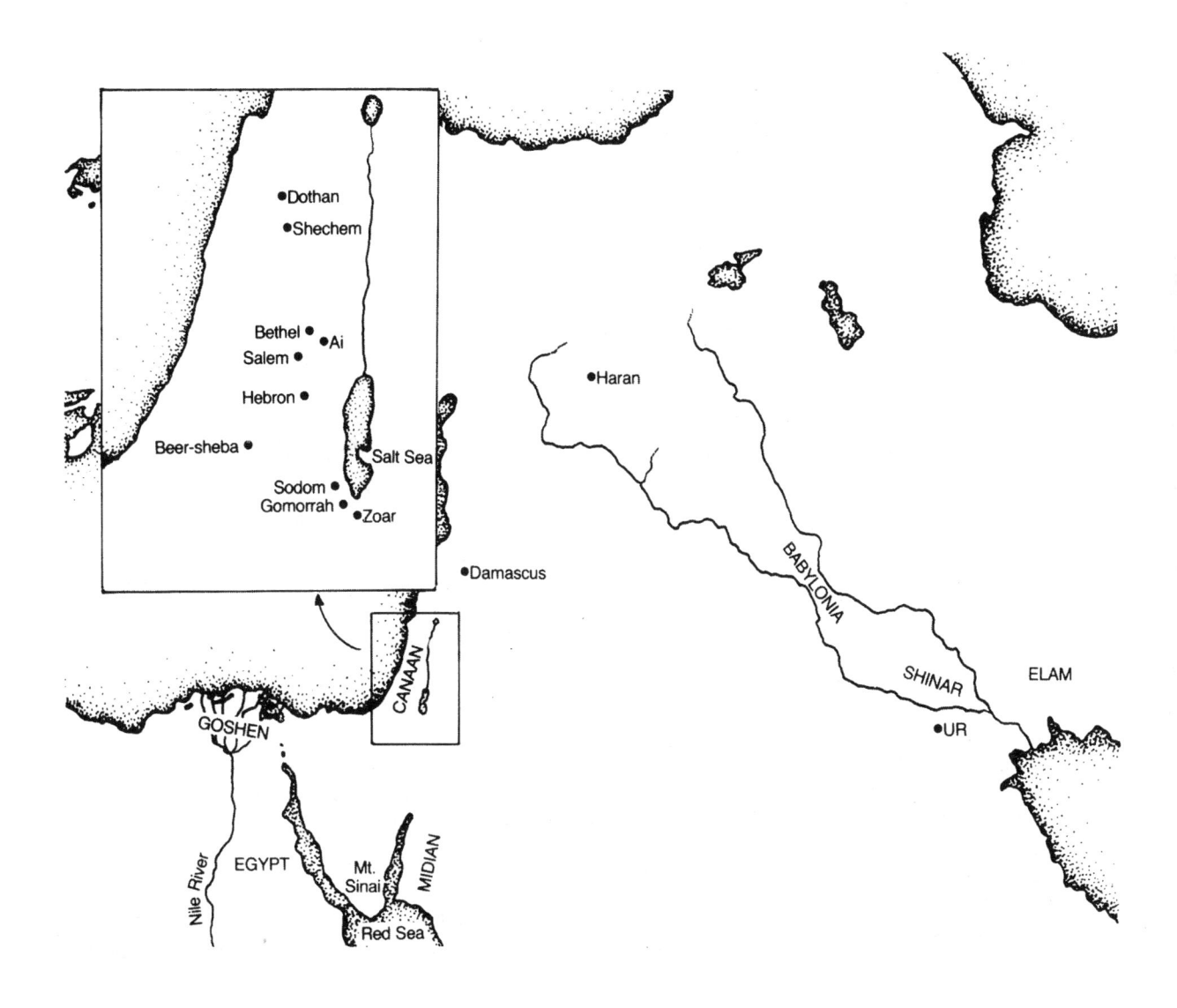

- Dothan
- Shechem
- Bethel
- Ai
- Salem
- Hebron
- Beer-sheba
- Salt Sea
- Sodom
- Gomorrah
- Zoar
- Damascus
- CANAAN
- GOSHEN
- Nile River
- EGYPT
- Mt. Sinai
- MIDIAN
- Red Sea
- Haran
- BABYLONIA
- SHINAR
- ELAM
- Ur

Reprinted from *The Bible Visual Resource Book*, © 1989 by Gospel Light Publications, Regal Books, Ventura, CA 93003. Used by permission.

THE EXODUS

The exodus and conquest narratives form the classic historical and spiritual drama of OT times. Subsequent ages looked back to this period as one of obedient and victorious living under divine guidance. Close examination of the environment and circumstances also reveals the strenuous exertions, human sin and bloody conflicts of the era.

Marah—Oasis
• Rameses—City or settlement
- - - → Trade routes
——→ Israelite route

Exact crossing place through the Biblical "Yam Suph" is unknown.

The Israelite tribes fled past the Egyptian system of border posts, through the Red Sea and into the desert, where they avoided the main military and trade routes leading across northern Sinai. The less frequently traveled "Way of the Sea" led to the remote turquoise and copper mining region northwest of Mt. Sinai.

It was necessary for Moses to take refuge in Midian where the Egyptian authorities could not reach him. The decades spent on "the far side of the desert" were an important formative part of his life.

In historical terms, the exodus from Egypt was ignored by Egyptian scribes and recorders. No definitive monuments mention the event itself, but a stele of Pharaoh Merneptah (c. 1225 B.C.) claims that a people called Israel were encountered by Egyptian troops somewhere in northern Canaan.

Finding precise geographical and chronological details of the period is problematic, but new information has emerged from vast amounts of fragmentary archaeological and inscriptional evidence. Hittite cuneiform documents parallel the ancient covenant formula governing Israel's "national contract" with God at Mount Sinai.

The Late Bronze Age (c. 1550-1200 B.C.) was a time of major social migrations. Egyptian control over the Semites in the eastern Nile delta was harsh, with a system of brickmaking quotas imposed on the labor force, often the landless, low-class "Apiru." Numerous Canaanite towns were violently destroyed. New populations, including the "Sea Peoples," made their presence felt in Anatolia, Egypt, Palestine, Transjordan, and elsewhere in the eastern Mediterranean.

Correspondence from Canaanite town rulers to the Egyptian court in the time of Akhenaten (c. 1375 B.C.) reveals a weak structure of alliances, with an intermittent Egyptian military presence and an ominous fear of people called "Habiru" ("Apiru").

Exodus 12:31—Deuteronomy 34:12
(Summary: Numbers 33:1-48)

Reprinted from *The Bible Visual Resource Book*, © 1989 by Gospel Light Publications, Regal Books, Ventura, CA 93003. Used by permission.

BIBLE LANDS

Black Sea

Caspian Sea

Mediterranean Sea

Red Sea

Persian Gulf

WHERE IT ALL HAPPENED

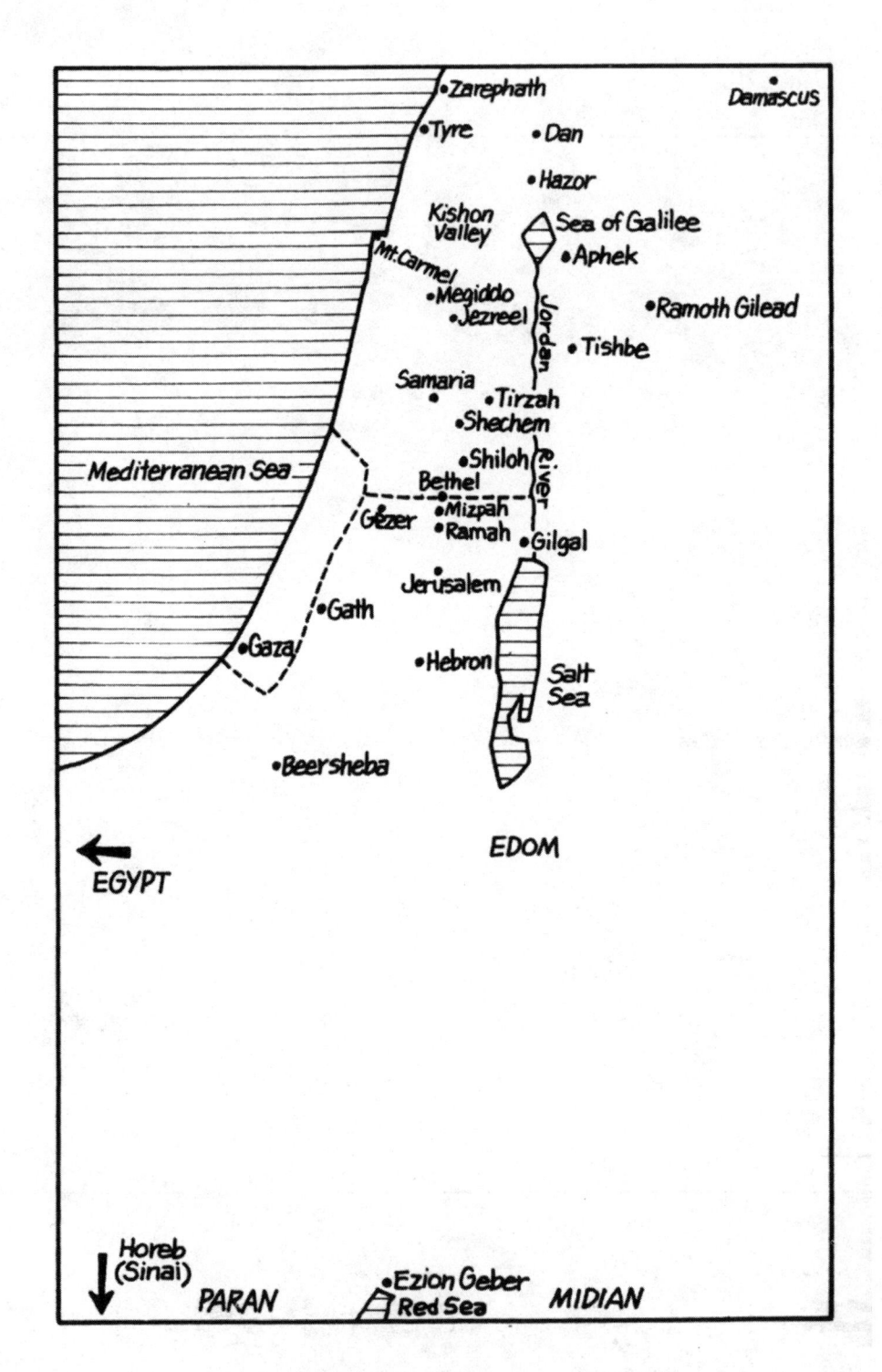

Reprinted from *What The Bible Is All About For Young Explorers*, © 1986 by Gospel Light Publications, Regal Books, Ventura, CA 93003. Used by permission.

MOSES & THE EXODUS

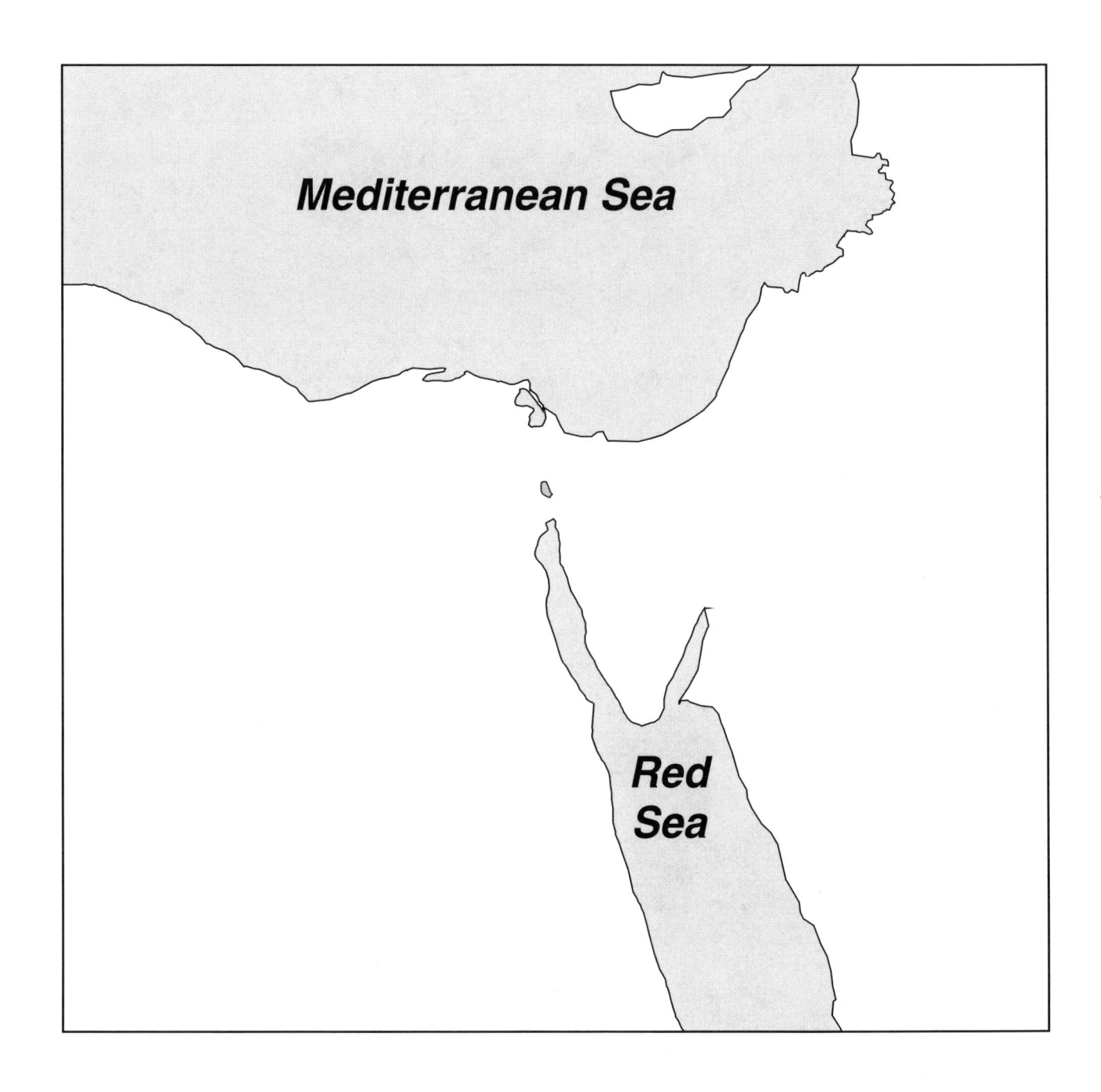

Mediterranean Sea

Red Sea

THE TABERNACLE

Exodus 35:30–36:38; 39:9–40:38

- Most Holy Place with the ark of the covenant 10 cubits square (*15 ft. square*)
- Curtain
- Holy Place, with the golden table for the bread of the Presence, golden lampstand, and altar of incense.
  - length: 20 cubits (*30 ft.*)
  - width: 10 cubits (*15 ft.*)
- 50 cubits
- 100 cubits (*150 ft. long*)
- Basin
- Bronze Altar
- Entrance 20 cubits (*30 ft. wide*)

The new religious observances taught by Moses in the desert centered on rituals connected with the tabernacle, and amplified Israel's sense of separateness, purity and oneness under the Lordship of Yahweh.

A few desert shrines have been found in Sinai, notably at Serabit el-Khadem and at Timnah in the Negev, and show marked Egyptian influence.

Specific cultural antecedents to portable shrines carried on poles and covered with thin sheets of gold can be found in ancient Egypt as early as the Old Kingdom (2800-2250 B.C.), but were especially prominent in the 18th and 19th dynasties (1570-1180). The best examples come from the fabulous tomb of Tutankhamun, c. 1350.

Comparisons of construction details in the text of Ex 25-40 with the frames, shrines, poles, sheathing, draped fabric covers, gilt rosettes, and winged protective figures from the shrine of Tutankhamun are instructive. The period, the Late Bronze Age, is equivalent in all dating systems to the era of Moses and the exodus.

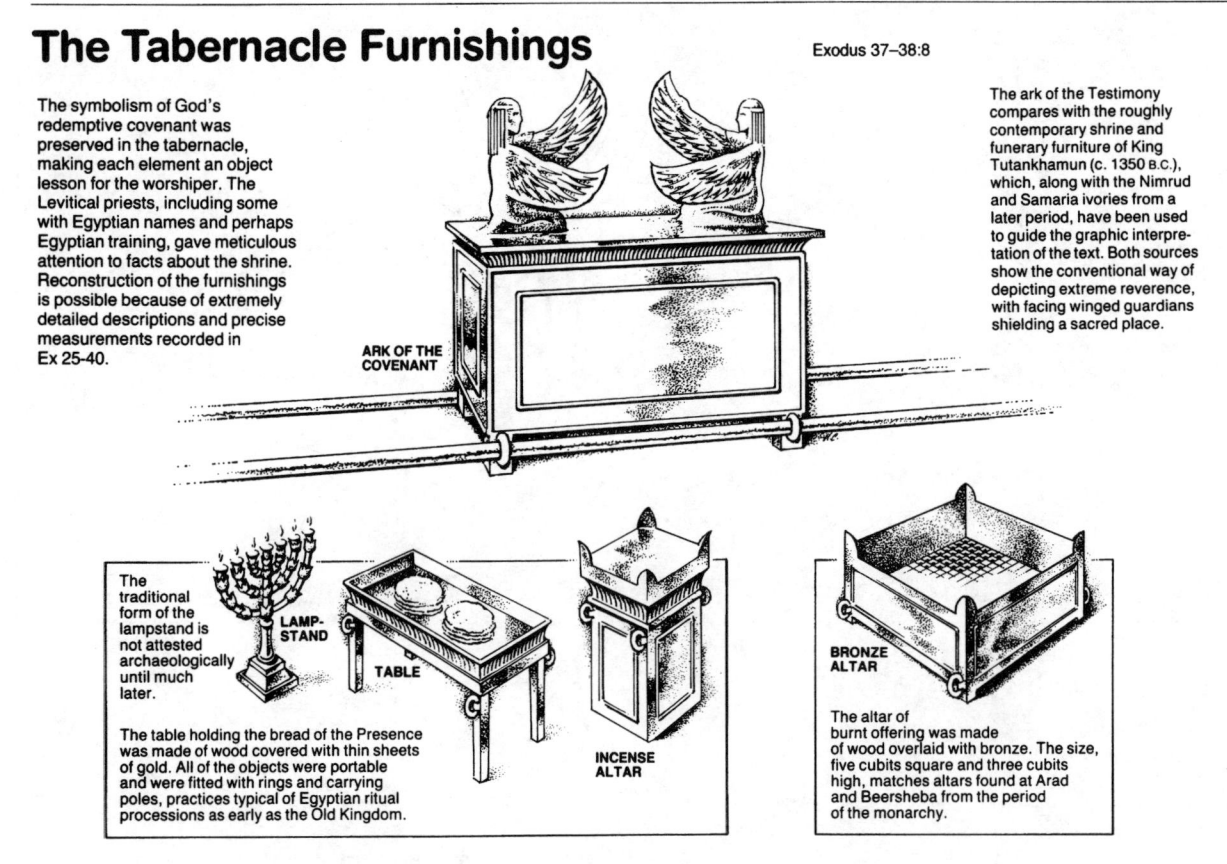

© Hugh Claycombe 1981

The Tabernacle Furnishings

Exodus 37–38:8

The symbolism of God's redemptive covenant was preserved in the tabernacle, making each element an object lesson for the worshiper. The Levitical priests, including some with Egyptian names and perhaps Egyptian training, gave meticulous attention to facts about the shrine. Reconstruction of the furnishings is possible because of extremely detailed descriptions and precise measurements recorded in Ex 25-40.

ARK OF THE COVENANT

The ark of the Testimony compares with the roughly contemporary shrine and funerary furniture of King Tutankhamun (c. 1350 B.C.), which, along with the Nimrud and Samaria ivories from a later period, have been used to guide the graphic interpretation of the text. Both sources show the conventional way of depicting extreme reverence, with facing winged guardians shielding a sacred place.

LAMPSTAND — The traditional form of the lampstand is not attested archaeologically until much later.

TABLE — The table holding the bread of the Presence was made of wood covered with thin sheets of gold. All of the objects were portable and were fitted with rings and carrying poles, practices typical of Egyptian ritual processions as early as the Old Kingdom.

INCENSE ALTAR

BRONZE ALTAR — The altar of burnt offering was made of wood overlaid with bronze. The size, five cubits square and three cubits high, matches altars found at Arad and Beersheba from the period of the monarchy.

Reprinted from *The Bible Visual Resource Book*, © 1989 by Gospel Light Publications, Regal Books, Ventura, CA 93003. Used by permission.

THE TEN COMMANDMENTS

1. You shall have no other gods before me

2. You shall not make for yourself an idol or bow down to them

3. You shall not misuse the name of the Lord your God

4. Remember the Sabbath day by keeping it holy

5. Honor your father and mother

6. You shall not murder

7. You shall not commit adultery

8. You shall not steal

9. You shall not give false testimony

10. You shall not covet

CONQUEST OF CANAAN

4. THE NORTHERN CAMPAIGN

Late Bronze Age Hazor was burned by Joshua (Jos 11:13). Excavations have revealed three clearly datable destruction layers, one of which may provide the strongest evidence yet for a historically verifiable date for the conquest.

The excavator thought Joshua burned the latest level (c. 1230 B.C.), but others argue that it must actually have been the earliest of the three levels, c. 1400 B.C.

1. ENTRY INTO CANAAN

When the Israelite tribes approached Canaan after four decades of desert existence, they had to overcome the two Amorite kingdoms on the Medeba plateau and in Bashan. Under Moses' leadership, they also subdued the Midianites in order to consolidate their control over the Transjordanian region.

The conquest of Canaan followed a course that in retrospect appears as though it had been planned by a brilliant strategist. Taking Jericho gave Israel control of its strategic plains, fords and roads as a base of operations. When Israel next gained control of the Bethel, Gibeon and the Upper Beth Horon region, she dominated the center of the north-south Palestinian ridge. Subsequently, she was able to break the power of the allied urban centers in separate campaigns south and north.

2. THE CENTRAL CAMPAIGN

The destruction of both Jericho and Ai led to a major victory against the Canaanites in the Valley of Aijalon—the "battle of the long day"—which then allowed Joshua to proceed against the cities of the western foothills.

Archaeological evidence for the conquest is mixed, in part because the chronological problems are unsolved. On the one hand, clay tablets containing cuneiform letters to the Egyptian court have been found at Tell el-Amarna in Egypt from c. 1375 B.C. These mention bands of *Habiru* who threaten many of the cities of Palestine and create fear among the Canaanite inhabitants.

On the other hand, numerous towns were destroyed c. 1230 B.C. by unknown assailants, presumably the "Sea Peoples," but possibly including the Israelites as well. The Biblical chronology based on 1Ki 6:1 seems to demand an even earlier dating, near the end of the 15th century (see Introduction to Joshua: Historical Setting).

3. THE SOUTHERN CAMPAIGN

Lachish, Debir, Libnah, Eglon and Makkedah (a town near Beth Shemesh and Azekah, whose exact location is unknown) were all captured by Joshua in his attack on the lowland foothills controlling the approaches to the Judahite plateau.

Several of these towns, most notably Lachish, contain destruction evidence that might possibly be correlated with the Israelite conquest, but with Jericho and Ai, the historical implications are not clear.

Reprinted from *The Bible Visual Resource Book*, © 1989 by Gospel Light Publications, Regal Books, Ventura, CA 93003. Used by permission.

JOSHUA ENTERING THE LAND OF CANAAN

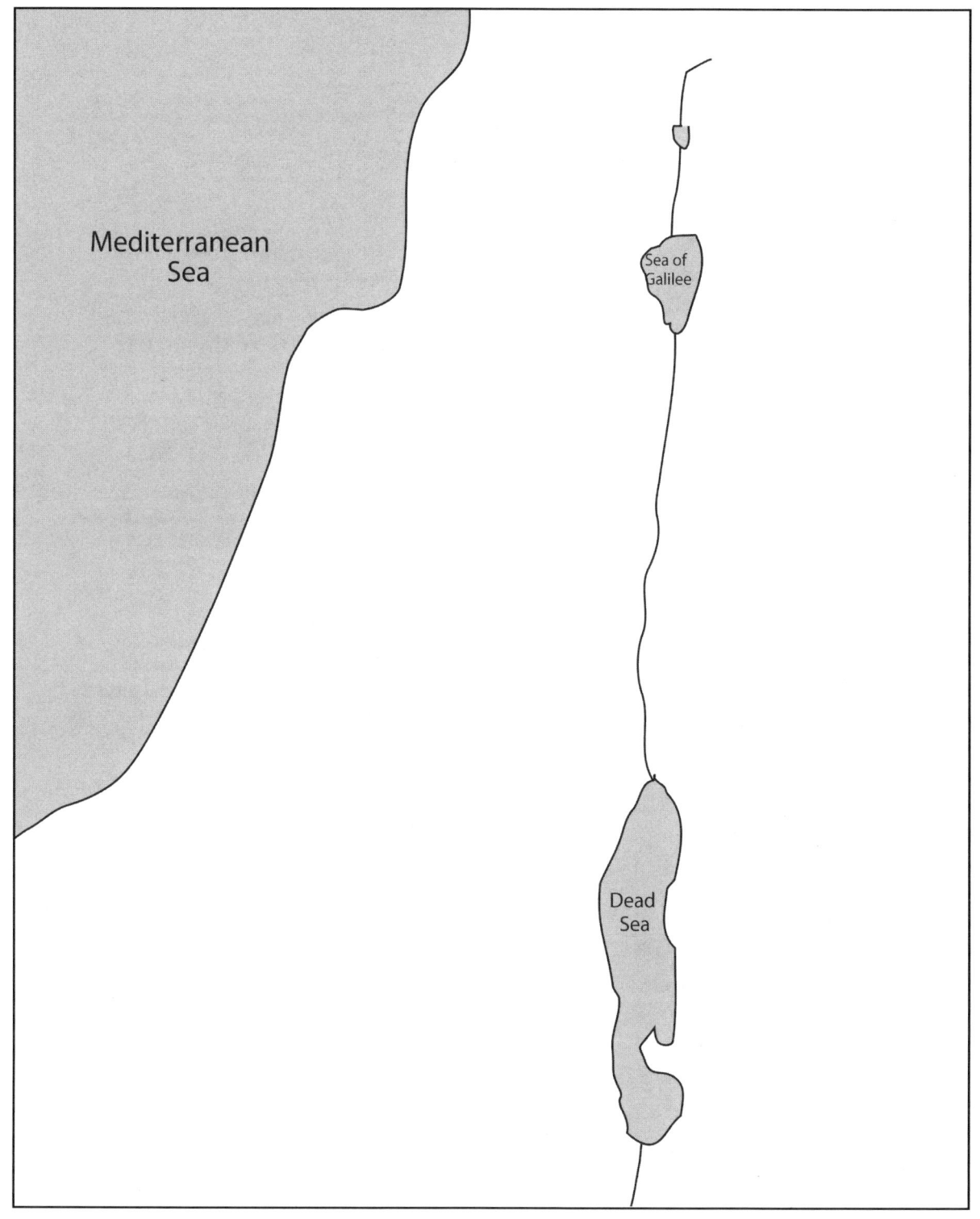

Mediterranean Sea

Sea of Galilee

Dead Sea

DAVID'S CONQUESTS

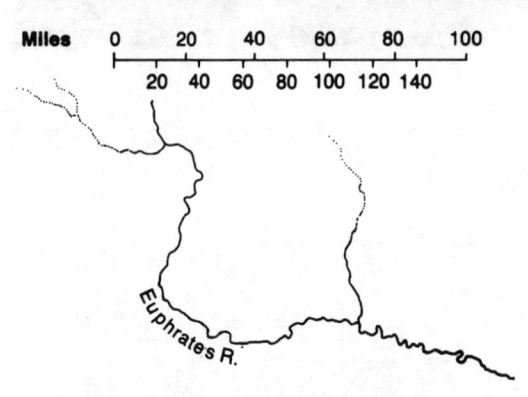

Once he had become king over all Israel (2Sa 5:1-5), David:

1. Conquered the Jebusite citadel of Zion/Jerusalem and made it his royal city (2Sa 5:6-10);

2. Received the recognition of and assurance of friendship from Hiram of Tyre, king of the Phoenicians (2Sa 5:11-12);

3. Decisively defeated the Philistines so that their hold on Israelite territory was broken and their threat to Israel eliminated (2Sa 5:17-25; 8:1);

4. Defeated the Moabites and imposed his authority over them (2Sa 8:2);

5. Crushed the Aramean kingdoms of Hadadezer (king of Zobah), Damascus and Maacah and put them under tribute (2Sa 8:3-8; 10:6-19). Talmai, the Aramean king of Geshur, apparently had made peace with David while he was still reigning in Hebron and sealed the alliance by giving his daughter in marriage to David (2Sa 3:3; see 1Ch 2:23);

6. Subdued Edom and incorporated it into his empire (2Sa 8:13-14);

7. Defeated the Ammonites and brought them into subjection (2Sa 12:19-31);

8. Subjugated the remaining Canaanite cities that had previously maintained their independence from and hostility toward Israel, such as Beth Shan, Megiddo, Taanach and Dor.

Since David had earlier crushed the Amalekites (1Sa 30:17), his wars thus completed the conquest begun by Joshua and secured all the borders of Israel. His empire (united Israel plus the subjugated kingdoms) reached from Ezion Geber on the eastern arm of the Red Sea to the Euphrates River.

Reprinted from *The Bible Visual Resource Book*, © 1989 by Gospel Light Publications, Regal Books, Ventura, CA 93003. Used by permission.

JERUSALEM

This diagram shows how Jerusalem grew in Old Testament times.

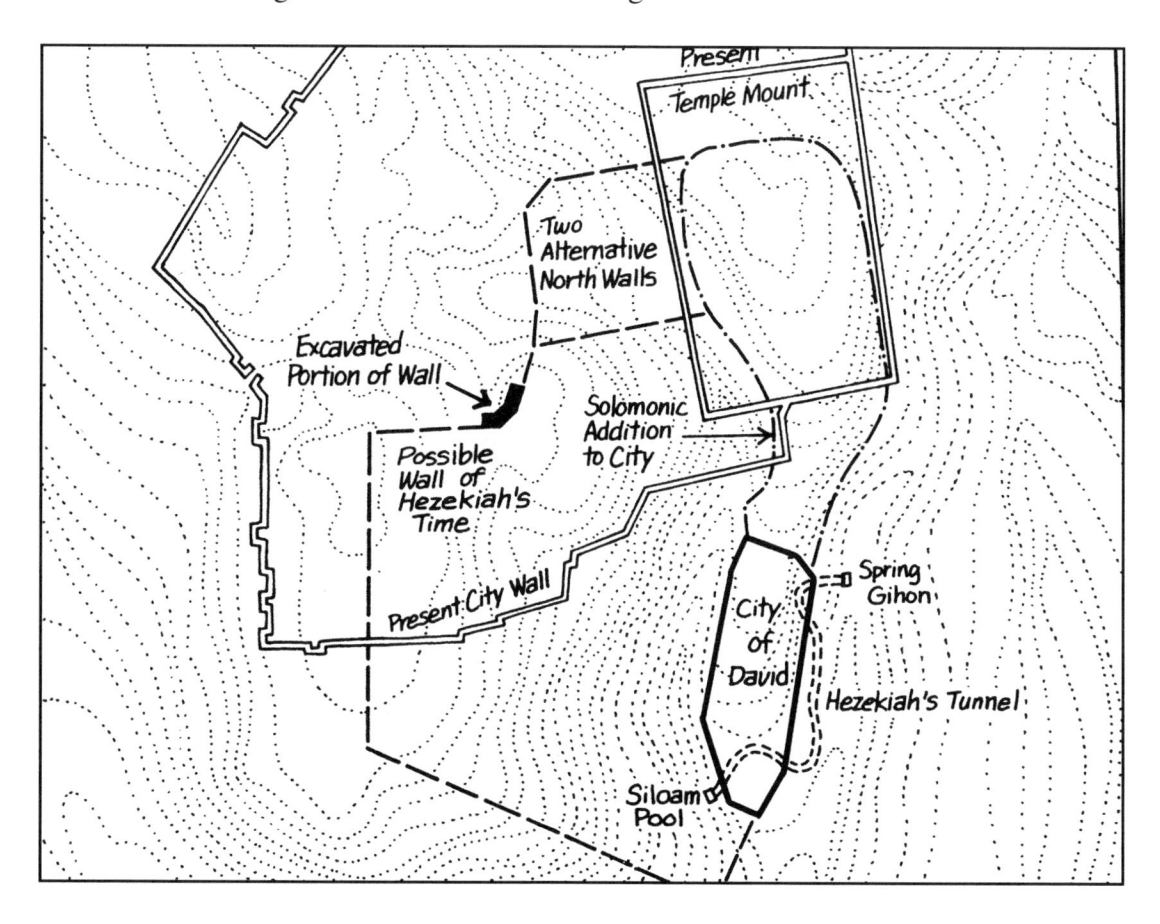

Reprinted from *What The Bible Is All About For Young Explorers*, © 1986 by Gospel Light Publications, Regal Books, Ventura, CA 93003. Used by permission.

TEMPLE

The Bible tells about three Temples built on the same spot, but at different times.

1. **The First Temple (Solomon's Temple)** was built under the leadership of King Solomon. When the Babylonians captured Jerusalem in 587 B.C., this Temple was destroyed.

2. **The Second Temple** was built by Jews who came back to Jerusalem after being captives in Babylon. (See Ezra.)

3. **Herod's Temple** was built over and around the existing Second Temple. It was destroyed in A.D. 70 by the Romans.

This is how Solomon's Temple looked.

Reprinted from *What The Bible Is All About For Young Explorers,* © 1986 by Gospel Light Publications, Regal Books, Ventura, CA 93003. Used by permission.

SOLOMON'S TEMPLE

960-586 B.C.

Temple source materials are subject to academic interpretation, and subsequent art reconstructions vary.

Most Holy Place with ark of the covenant

Holy Place (30 cubits high) with golden tables for bread of the Presence, gold lampstands, and altar of incense.

Side rooms

Portico

The ornate cast bronze pillars, "Jakin and Boaz"

Movable stands of bronze

Sea

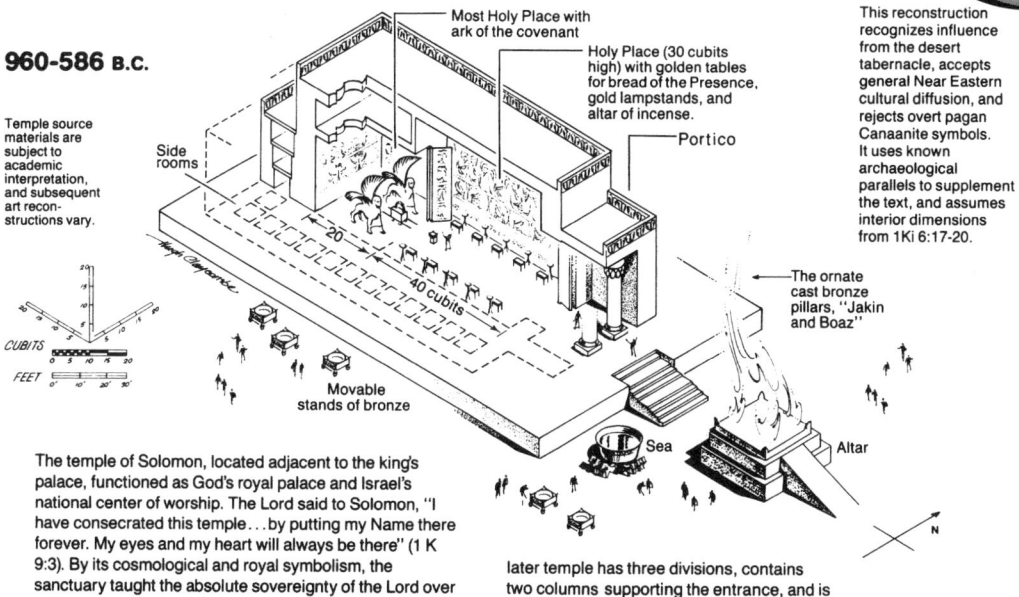

Altar

This reconstruction recognizes influence from the desert tabernacle, accepts general Near Eastern cultural diffusion, and rejects overt pagan Canaanite symbols. It uses known archaeological parallels to supplement the text, and assumes interior dimensions from 1Ki 6:17-20.

The temple of Solomon, located adjacent to the king's palace, functioned as God's royal palace and Israel's national center of worship. The Lord said to Solomon, "I have consecrated this temple...by putting my Name there forever. My eyes and my heart will always be there" (1 K 9:3). By its cosmological and royal symbolism, the sanctuary taught the absolute sovereignty of the Lord over the whole creation and his special headship over Israel.

The floor plan is a type that has a long history in Semitic religion, particularly among the West Semites. An early example of the tripartite division into *'ulam, hekal,* and *debir* (portico, main hall, and inner sanctuary) has been found at Syrian Ebla (c. 2300 B.C.) and, much later but more contemporaneous with Solomon, at Tell Tainat in the Orontes basin (c. 900 B.C.). Like Solomon's, the later temple has three divisions, contains two columns supporting the entrance, and is located adjacent to the royal palace.

Many archaeological parallels can be drawn to the methods of construction used in the temple, e.g., the "stone and cedar beam" technique described in 1Ki 6:36. Interestingly, evidence for the largest bronze-casting industry ever found in Palestine comes from the same locale and period as that indicated in Scripture: Zarethan in the Jordan Valley c. 1000 B.C.

© Hugh Claycombe 1986

Temple Furnishings

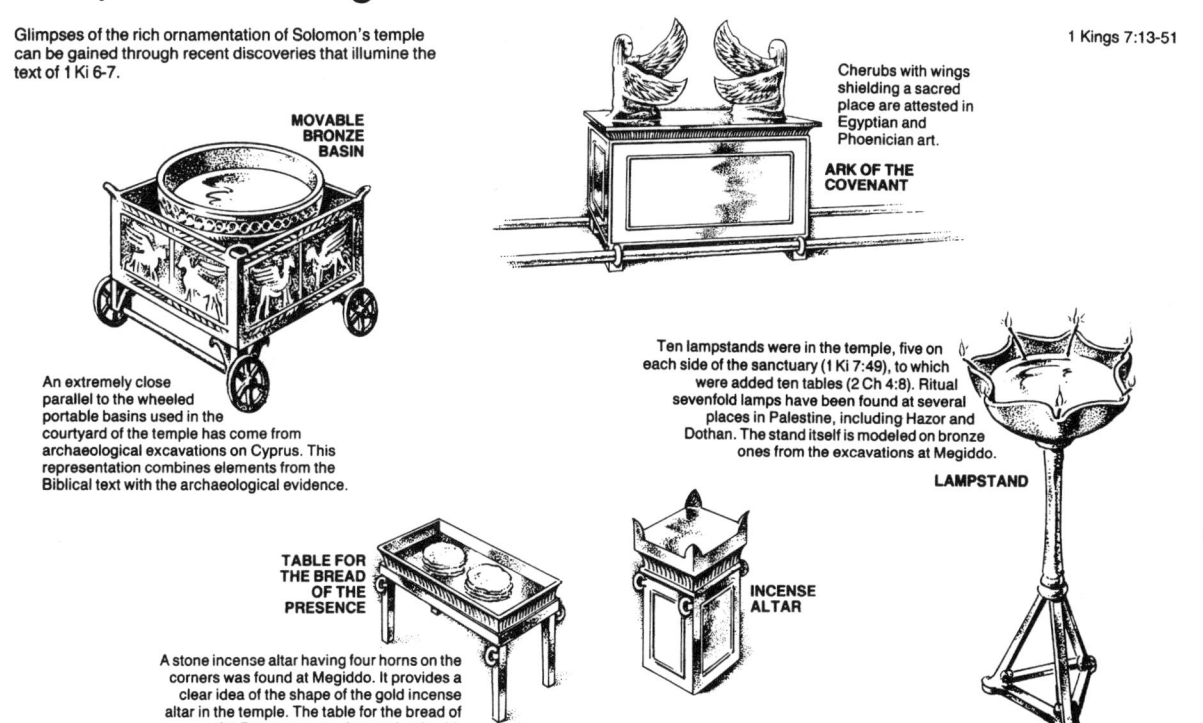

Glimpses of the rich ornamentation of Solomon's temple can be gained through recent discoveries that illumine the text of 1 Ki 6-7.

1 Kings 7:13-51

MOVABLE BRONZE BASIN

An extremely close parallel to the wheeled portable basins used in the courtyard of the temple has come from archaeological excavations on Cyprus. This representation combines elements from the Biblical text with the archaeological evidence.

Cherubs with wings shielding a sacred place are attested in Egyptian and Phoenician art.

ARK OF THE COVENANT

Ten lampstands were in the temple, five on each side of the sanctuary (1 Ki 7:49), to which were added ten tables (2 Ch 4:8). Ritual sevenfold lamps have been found at several places in Palestine, including Hazor and Dothan. The stand itself is modeled on bronze ones from the excavations at Megiddo.

LAMPSTAND

TABLE FOR THE BREAD OF THE PRESENCE

INCENSE ALTAR

A stone incense altar having four horns on the corners was found at Megiddo. It provides a clear idea of the shape of the gold incense altar in the temple. The table for the bread of the Presence was also made of gold.

Reprinted from *The Bible Visual Resource Book*, © 1989 by Gospel Light Publications, Regal Books, Ventura, CA 93003. Used by permission.